Ballads of a Cheechako

You are holding a reproduction of an original work that is in the public domain in the United States of America, and possibly other countries. You may freely copy and distribute this work as no entity (individual or corporate) has a copyright on the body of the work. This book may contain prior copyright references, and library stamps (as most of these works were scanned from library copies). These have been scanned and retained as part of the historical artifact.

This book may have occasional imperfections such as missing or blurred pages, poor pictures, errant marks, etc. that were either part of the original artifact, or were introduced by the scanning process. We believe this work is culturally important, and despite the imperfections, have elected to bring it back into print as part of our continuing commitment to the preservation of printed works worldwide. We appreciate your understanding of the imperfections in the preservation process, and hope you enjoy this valuable book.

BALLADS OF A CHEECHAKO

BALLADS OF A CHEECHAKO

BY
ROBERT W. SERVICE

AUTHOR OF
"SONGS OF A SOURDOUGH"

TORONTO
WILLIAM BRIGGS
1911

To the Man of the High North

MY rhymes are rough, and often in my rhyming
  I've drifted, silver-sailed, on seas of dream,
Hearing afar the bells of Elfland chiming,
  Seeing the groves of Arcadie agleam.

I was the thrall of Beauty that rejoices
  From peak snow-diademed to regal star;
Yet to mine aerie ever pierced the voices,
  The pregnant voices of the Things That Are.

The Here, the Now, the vast Forlorn around us;
  The gold-delirium, the ferine strife;
The lusts that lure us on, the hates that hound
    us;
  Our red rags in the patch-work quilt of Life.

TO THE MAN OF THE HIGH NORTH

The nameless men who nameless rivers travel,
  And in strange valleys greet strange deaths
    alone;
The grim, intrepid ones who would unravel
  The mysteries that shroud the Polar Zone.

These will I sing, and if one of you linger
  Over my pages in the Long, Long Night,
And on some lone line lay a calloused finger,
  Saying: "It's human-true—it hits me right:"
Then will I count this loving toil well spent;
Then will I dream awhile—content, content.

CONTENTS

	PAGE
TO THE MAN OF THE HIGH NORTH	v

"My rhymes are rough, and often in my rhyming."

MEN OF THE HIGH NORTH 15

"Men of the High North, the wild sky is blazing."

THE BALLAD OF THE NORTHERN LIGHTS 18

"One of the Down and Out—that's me. Stare at me well, ay, stare!"

THE BALLAD OF THE BLACK FOX SKIN . 33

"There was Claw-fingered Kitty and Windy Ike living the life of shame."

THE BALLAD OF PIOUS PETE 43

"I tried to refine that neighbor of mine, honest to God, I did."

THE BALLAD OF BLASPHEMOUS BILL . . 50

"I took a contract to bury the body of blasphemous Bill MacKie."

THE BALLAD OF ONE-EYED MIKE 57

"This is the tale that was told to me by the man with the crystal eye."

CONTENTS

	PAGE
THE BALLAD OF THE BRAND.	62

"'Twas up in a land long famed for gold, where women were far and rare."

THE BALLAD OF HARD-LUCK HENRY . . 71

"Now wouldn't you expect to find a man an awful crank."

THE BALLAD OF GUM-BOOT BEN 76

"He was an old prospector with a vision bleared and dim."

THE MAN FROM ELDORADO 81

"He's the man from Eldorado, and he's just arrived in town."

MY FRIENDS 90

"The man above was a murderer, the man below was a thief."

THE PROSPECTOR 94

"I strolled up old Bonanza, where I staked in ninety-eight."

THE BLACK SHEEP 100

"Hark to the ewe that bore him."

THE TELEGRAPH OPERATOR 105

"I will not wash my face."

THE WOOD-CUTTER 109

"The sky is like an envelope."

CONTENTS

	PAGE
THE SONG OF THE MOUTH-ORGAN	114

"I'm a homely little bit of tin and bone."

THE TRAIL OF NINETY-EIGHT 118
"Gold! We leapt from our benches. Gold! We sprang from our stools."

CLANCY OF THE MOUNTED POLICE . . . 128
"In the little Crimson Manual it's written plain and clear."

LOST 138
"Black is the sky, but the land is white."

L'ENVOI 145
"We talked of yesteryears, of trails and treasure."

ILLUSTRATIONS

	PAGE
"Your little sod-roofed cabins with the snugly moss-chinked walls" . . . . *Frontispiece*	
"Beauty that rejoices from peak snow-diademed to regal star"	18
"O'er soundless lakes where the grayling makes a rush at the clumsy fly"	32
"The vastitudes where the world protrudes through clouds like seas up-shoaled" . . .	42
"For once you've panned the speckled sand, and seen the bonny dust"	56
"The big, blue, silt-freighted Yukon"	70
"The lonely waif of the wood-camp"	90
"Nothing but rock and tree; nothing but wood and stone"	104
"We tightened our girths and our pack-straps; we linked on the Human Chain"	120
"There was the rage of the rapids"	138

BALLADS OF A CHEECHAKO

Men of the High North

Men of the High North, the wild sky is blazing;
    Islands of opal float on silver seas;
Swift splendors kindle, barbaric, amazing;
    Pale ports of amber, golden argosies.
Ringed all around us the proud peaks are glow‑
    ing;
    Fierce chiefs in council, their wigwam the sky;
Far, far below us the big Yukon flowing,
    Like threaded quicksilver, gleams to the eye.

Men of the High North, you who have known it;
    You in whose hearts its splendors have abode;
Can you renounce it, can you disown it?
    Can you forget it, its glory and its goad?
Where is the hardship, where is the pain of it?
    Lost in the limbo of things you've forgot;
Only remain the guerdon and gain of it,
    Zest of the foray—and God, how you fought!

You who have made good, you foreign faring;
  You money magic to far lands has whirled;
Can you forget those days of vast daring,
  There with your soul on the Top o' the World?
Nights when no peril could keep you awake on
  Spruce boughs you spread for your couch in
    the snow;
Taste all your feasts like the beans and the bacon
  Fried at the camp-fire at forty below?

Can you remember your huskies all going,
  Barking with joy and their brushes in air;
You in your parki, glad-eyed and glowing,
  Monarch, your subjects the wolf and the bear?
Monarch, your kingdom unravisht and gleaming;
  Mountains your throne, and a river your car;
Crash of a bull moose to rouse you from dream-
    ing;
  Forest your couch, and your candle a star.

  You who this faint day the High North is luring
    Unto her vastness, taintlessly sweet;
  You who are steel-braced, straight-lipped, en-
      during,
    Dreadless in danger and dire in defeat:

Men of the High North

Honor the High North ever and evèr,
  Whether she crown you, or whether she slay;
Suffer her fury, cherish and love her—
  He who would rule he must learn to obey.

Men of the High North, fierce mountains love
      you;
  Proud rivers leap when you ride on their
      breast.
See, the austere sky, pensive above you,
  Dons all her jewels to smile on your rest.
Children of Freedom, scornful of frontiers,
  We who are weaklings honor your worth.
Lords of the wilderness, Princes of Pioneers,
  Let's have a rouse that will ring round the
      earth.

The Ballad of the Northern Lights

One of the Down and Out—that's me. Stare at
    me well, ay, stare!
Stare and shrink—say! you wouldn't think that
    I was a millionaire.
Look at my face, it's crimped and gouged—one
    of them death-mask things;
Don't seem the sort of man, do I, as might be
    the pal of kings?
Slouching along in smelly rags, a bleary-eyed,
    no-good bum;
A knight of the hollow needle, pard, spewed
    from the sodden slum.
Look me all over from head to foot; how much
    would you think I was worth?
A dollar? a dime? a nickel? Why, *I'm the
    wealthiest man on earth.*

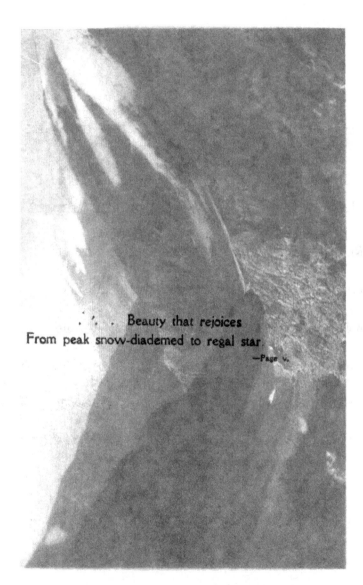

. . . Beauty that rejoices
From peak snow-diademed to regal star.
—Page v.

Stare and shrink—say! you wouldn't think that
    I was once the sort of man, do I, as might be
    the pal of kings?
Slouching along in smelly rags, a bleary-eyed,
    no-good bum;
A knight of the hollow needle, pard, spewed
    from the sodden slum.
Look me all over from head to foot; how much
    would you think I was worth?

The Ballad of the Northern Lights

No, don't you think that I'm off my base. You'll
    sing a different tune
If only you'll let me spin my yarn. Come over
    to this saloon;
Wet my throat—it's as dry as chalk, and seeing
    as how it's you,
I'll tell the tale of a Northern trail, and so help
    me God, it's true.
I'll tell of the howling wilderness and the hag-
    gard arctic heights,
Of a reckless vow that I made, and how *I staked
    the Northern Lights*.

Remember the year of the Big Stampede and the
    Trail of Ninety-eight,
When the eyes of the world were turned to the
    North, and the hearts of men elate;
Hearts of the old dare-devil breed thrilled at the
    wondrous strike,
And to every man who could hold a pan came
    the message, "Up and hike."
Well, I was there with the best of them, and I
    knew I would not fail.
You wouldn't believe it to see me now; but wait
    till you've heard my tale.

You've read of the Trail of Ninety-eight, but its
    woe no man may tell;
It was all of a piece and a whole yard wide, and
    the name of the brand was " Hell."
We heard the call and we staked our all; we
    were plungers playing blind,
And no man cared how his neighbor fared, and
    no man looked behind;
For a ruthless greed was born of need, and the
    weakling went to the wall,
And a curse might avail where a prayer would
    fail, and the gold-lust crazed us all.

Bold were we, and they called us three the " Unholy Trinity;"
There was Ole Olson, the sailor Swede, and the
    Dago Kid and me.
We were the discards of the pack, the foreloopers
    of Unrest,
Reckless spirits of fierce revolt in the ferment
    of the West.
We were bound to win and we revelled in the
    hardships of the way.
We staked our ground and our hopes were
    crowned, and we hoisted out the pay.
We were rich in a day beyond our dreams, it was
    gold from the grass-roots down;

The Ballad of the Northern Lights

But we weren't used to such sudden wealth, and there was the siren town.
We were crude and careless frontiersmen, with much in us of the beast;
We could bear the famine worthily, but we lost our heads at the feast.
The town looked mighty bright to us, with a bunch of dust to spend,
And nothing was half too good them days, and everyone was our friend.
Wining meant more than mining then, and life was a dizzy whirl,
Gambling and dropping chunks of gold down the neck of a dance-hall girl;
Till we went clean mad, it seems to me, and we squandered our last poke,
And we sold our claim, and we found ourselves one bitter morning—broke.

The Dago Kid he dreamed a dream of his mother's aunt who died—
In the dawn-light dim she came to him, and she stood by his bedside,
And she said: "Go forth to the highest North till a lonely trail ye find;
Follow it far and trust your star, and fortune will be kind."

But I jeered at him, and then there came the
    Sailor Swede to me,
And he said: "I dreamed of my sister's son, who
    croaked at the age of three.
From the herded dead he sneaked and said:
    'Seek you an Arctic trail;
'Tis pale and grim by the Polar rim, but seek and
    ye shall not fail.'"
And lo! that night I too did dream of my
    mother's sister's son,
And he said to me: "By the Arctic Sea there's
    a treasure to be won.
Follow and follow a lone moose trail, till you
    come to a valley grim,
On the slope of the lonely watershed that borders
    the Polar brim."
Then I woke my pals, and soft we swore by the
    mystic Silver Flail,
'Twas the hand of Fate, and to-morrow straight
    we would seek the lone moose trail.

We watched the groaning ice wrench free, crash
    on with a hollow din;
Men of the wilderness were we, freed from the
    taint of sin.
The mighty river snatched us up and it bore us
    swift along;

The days were bright, and the morning light was sweet with jewelled song.
We poled and lined up nameless streams, portaged o'er hill and plain;
We burnt our boat to save the nails, and built our boat again;
We guessed and groped, North, ever North, with many a twist and turn;
We saw ablaze in the deathless days the splendid sunsets burn.
O'er soundless lakes where the grayling makes a rush at the clumsy fly;
By bluffs so steep that the hard-hit sheep falls sheer from out the sky;
By lilied pools where the bull moose cools and wallows in huge content;
By rocky lairs where the pig-eyed bears peered at our tiny tent.
Through the black canyon's angry foam we hurled to dreamy bars,
And round in a ring the dog-nosed peaks bayed to the mocking stars.
Spring and summer and autumn went; the sky had a tallow gleam,
Yet North and ever North we pressed to the land of our Golden Dream.

So we came at last to a tundra vast, and dark and grim and lone,
And there was the little lone moose trail, and we knew it for our own.
By muskeg hollow and nigger-head it wandered endlessly;
Sorry of heart and sore of foot, weary men were we.
The short-lived sun had a leaden glare and the darkness came too soon,
And stationed there with a solemn stare was the pinched, anaemic moon.
Silence and silvern solitude till it made you dumbly shrink,
And you thought to hear with an outward ear the things you thought to think.

Oh, it was wild and weird and wan, and ever in camp o' nights
We would watch and watch the silver dance of the mystic Northern Lights.
And soft they danced from the Polar sky and swept in primrose haze;
And swift they pranced with their silver feet, and pierced with a blinding blaze.
They danced a cotillion in the sky; they were rose and silver shod;

The Ballad of the Northern Lights

It was not good for the eyes of man—'twas a
 sight for the eyes of God.
It made us mad and strange and sad, and the
 gold whereof we dreamed
Was all forgot, and our only thought was of the
 lights that gleamed.

Oh, the tundra sponge it was golden brown, and
 some was a bright blood-red;
And the reindeer moss gleamed here and there
 like the tombstones of the dead.
And in and out and around about the little trail
 ran clear,
And we hated it with a deadly hate and we
 feared with a deadly fear.
And the skies of night were alive with light, with
 a throbbing, thrilling flame;
Amber and rose and violet, opal and gold it came.
It swept the sky like a giant scythe, it quivered
 back to a wedge;
Argently bright, it cleft the night with a wavy
 golden edge.
Pennants of silver waved and streamed, lazy
 banners unfurled;
Sudden splendors of sabres gleamed, lightning
 javelins were hurled.

There in our awe we crouched and saw with our
 wild, uplifted eyes
Charge and retire the hosts of fire in the battle-
 field of the skies.

But all things come to an end at last, and the
 muskeg melted away,
And frowning down to bar our path a muddle of
 mountains lay.
And a gorge sheered up in granite walls, and the
 moose trail crept betwixt—
'Twas as if the earth had gaped too far and her
 stony jaws were fixt.
Then the winter fell with a sudden swoop, and
 the heavy clouds sagged low,
And earth and sky were blotted out in a whirl
 of driving snow.

We were climbing up a glacier in the neck of a
 mountain pass,
When the Dago Kid slipped down and fell into
 a deep crevasse.
When we got him out one leg hung limp, and his
 brow was wreathed with pain,
And he says: " 'Tis badly broken, boys, and I'll
 never walk again.

The Ballad of the Northern Lights

It's death for all if ye linger here, and that's no
    cursèd lie;
Go on, go on while the trail is good, and leave
    me down to die."
He raved and swore, but we tended him with our
    uncouth, clumsy care.
The camp-fire gleamed and he gazed and dreamed
    with a fixed and curious stare.
Then all at once he grabbed my gun and he put
    it to his head,
And he says: " I'll fix it for you, boys "—them
    are the words he said.

So we sewed him up in a canvas sack and we
    slung him to a tree;
And the stars like needles stabbed our eyes, and
    woeful men were we.
And on we went on our woeful way, wrapped in
    a daze of dream,
And the Northern Lights in the crystal nights
    came forth with a mystic gleam.
They danced and they danced the devil-dance
    over the naked snow;
And soft they rolled like a tide upshoaled with a
    ceaseless ebb and flow.
They rippled green with a wondrous sheen, they
    fluttered out like a fan;

They spread with a blaze of rose-pink rays never
 yet seen of man.
They writhed like a brood of angry snakes, hiss-
 ing and sulphur-pale;
Then swift they changed to a dragon vast, lashing a cloven tail.
It seemed to us, as we gazed aloft with an ever-
 lasting stare,
The sky was a pit of bale and dread, and a
 monster revelled there.

We climbed the rise of a hog-back range that was
 desolate and drear,
When the Sailor Swede had a crazy fit, and he
 got to talking queer.
He talked of his home in Oregon and the peach
 trees all in bloom,
And the fern head-high, and the topaz sky, and
 the forest's scented gloom.
He talked of the sins of his misspent life, and
 then he seemed to brood,
And I watched him there like a fox a hare, for I
 knew it was not good.
And sure enough in the dim dawn light I missed
 him from the tent,
And a fresh trail broke through the crusted
 snow, and I knew not where it went.

But I followed it o'er the seamless waste, and I
 found him at shut of day,
Naked there as a new-born babe—so I left him
 where he lay.

Day after day was sinister, and I fought fierce-
 eyed despair,
And I clung to life, and I struggled on, I knew
 not why nor where.
I packed my grub in short relays, and I cowered
 down in my tent,
And the world around was purged of sound like
 a frozen continent.
Day after day was dark as death, but ever and
 ever at nights,
With a brilliancy that grew and grew, blazed up
 the Northern Lights.
They rolled around with a soundless sound like
 softly bruisèd silk;
They poured into the bowl of the sky with the
 gentle flow of milk.
In eager, pulsing violet their wheeling chariots
 came,
Or they poised above the Polar rim like a coronal
 of flame.
From depths of darkness fathomless their lancing
 rays were hurled,

Like the all-combining search-lights of the navies of the world.
There on the roof-pole of the world as one bewitched I gazed,
And howled and grovelled like a beast as the awful splendors blazed.
My eyes were seared, yet thralled I peered through the parki hood nigh blind;
But I staggered on to the lights that shone, and never I looked behind.

There is a mountain round and low that lies by the Polar rim,
And I climbed its height in a whirl of light, and I peered o'er its jagged brim;
And there in a crater deep and vast, ungained, unguessed of men,
The mystery of the Arctic world was flashed into my ken.
For there these poor dim eyes of mine beheld the sight of sights—
That hollow ring was the source and spring of the mystic Northern Lights.

Then I staked that place from crown to base, and I hit the homeward trail.

The Ballad of the Northern Lights

Ah, God! it was good, though my eyes were
    blurred, and I crawled like a sickly snail.
In that vast white world where the silent sky
    communes with the silent snow,
In hunger and cold and misery I wandered to
    and fro.
But the Lord took pity on my pain, and He led
    me to the sea,
And some ice-bound whalers heard my moan, and
    they fed and sheltered me.
They fed the feeble scarecrow thing that
    stumbled out of the wild
With the ravaged face of a mask of death and
    the wandering wits of a child—
A craven, cowering bag of bones that once had
    been a man.
They tended me and they brought me back to
    the world, and here I am.

Some say that the Northern Lights are the glare
    of the Arctic ice and snow;
And some that it's electricity, and nobody seems
    to know.
But I'll tell you now—and if I lie, may my lips
    be stricken dumb—
It's a *mine*, a mine of the precious stuff that men
    call radium.

It's a million dollars a pound, they say, and there's tons and tons in sight.
You can see it gleam in a golden stream in the solitudes of night.
And it's mine, all mine—and say! if you have a hundred plunks to spare,
I'll let you have the chance of your life, I'll sell you a quarter share.
You turn it down? Well, I'll make it ten, seeing as you are my friend.
Nothing doing? Say! don't be hard—have you got a dollar to lend?
Just a dollar to help me out, I know you'll treat me white;
I'll do as much for you some day . . . God bless you, sir; good-night.

The Ballad of the Black Fox Skin

I.

THERE was Claw-fingered Kitty and Windy Ike
    living the life of shame,
When unto them in the Long, Long Night came
    the man-who-had-no-name;
Bearing his prize of a black fox pelt, out of the
    Wild he came.

His cheeks were blanched as the flume-head foam
    when the brown spring freshets flow;
Deep in their dark, sin-calcined pits were his
    sombre eyes aglow;
They knew him far for the fitful man who spat
    forth blood on the snow.

"Did ever you see such a skin?" quoth he;
 "there's nought in the world so fine—
Such fullness of fur, as black as the night, such
 lustre, such size, such shine;
It's life to a one-lunged man like me; it's London,
 it's women, it's wine.

"The Moose-hides called it the devil-fox, and
 swore that no man could kill;
That he who hunted it, soon or late, must surely
 suffer some ill;
But I laughed at them and their old squaw-
 tales. Ha! ha! I'm laughing still.

"For, look ye, the skin—it's as smooth as sin,
 and black as the core of the Pit.
By gun or by trap, whatever the hap, I swore I
 would capture it;
By star and by star afield and afar, I hunted
 and would not quit.

"For the devil-fox it was swift and sly, and it
 seemed to fleer at me;
I would wake in fright by the camp-fire light,
 hearing its evil glee;
Into my dream its eyes would gleam, and its
 shadow would I see.

The Ballad of the Black Fox Skin

"It sniffed and ran from the ptarmigan I had
    poisoned to excess;
Unharmed it sped from my wrathful lead ('twas
    as if I shot by guess);
Yet it came by night in the stark moonlight to
    mock at my weariness.

"I tracked it up where the mountains hunch
    like the vertebrae of the world;
I tracked it down to the death-still pits where the
    avalanche is hurled;
From the glooms to the sacerdotal snows, where
    the carded clouds are curled.

"From the vastitudes where the world protrudes
    through clouds like seas up-shoaled,
I held its track till it led me back to the land I
    had left of old—
The land I had looted many moons. I was weary
    and sick and cold.

"I was sick, soul-sick, of the futile chase, and
    there and then I swore
The foul fiend fox might scathless go, for I
    would hunt no more;
Then I rubbed mine eyes in a vast surprise—it
    stood by my cabin door.

"A rifle raised in the wraith-like gloom, and a
    vengeful shot that sped;
A howl that would thrill a cream-faced corpse—
    and the demon fox lay dead. . . .
Yet there was never a sign of wound, and never
    a drop he bled.

" So that was the end of the great black fox, and
    here is the prize I've won;
And now for a drink to cheer me up—I've
    mushed since the early sun;
We'll drink a toast to the sorry ghost of the fox
    whose race is run."

II.

Now Claw-fingered Kitty and Windy Ike, bad as
    the worst were they;
In their road-house down by the river-trail they
    waited and watched for prey;
With wine and song they joyed night long, and
    they slept like swine by day.

For things were done in the Midnight Sun that
    no tongue will ever tell;
And men there be who walk earth-free, but whose
    names are writ in Hell—
Are writ in flames with the guilty names of
    Fournier and Labelle.

The Ballad of the Black Fox Skin

Put not your trust in a poke of dust would ye
    sleep the sleep of sin;
For there be those who would rob your clothes
    ere yet the dawn comes in;
And a prize likewise in a woman's eyes is a peer-
    less black fox skin.

Put your faith in the mountain cat if you lie
    within his lair;
Trust the fangs of the mother-wolf, and the claws
    of the lead-ripped bear;
But oh, of the wiles and the gold-tooth smiles of
    a dance-hall wench beware!

Wherefore it was beyond all laws that lusts of
    man restrain,
A man drank deep and sank to sleep, never to
    wake again;
And the Yukon swallowed through a hole the
    cold corpse of the slain.

III.

The black fox skin a shadow cast from the roof
    nigh to the floor;
And sleek it seemed and soft it gleamed, and the
    woman stroked it o'er;
And the man stood by with a brooding eye, and
    gnashed his teeth and swore.

When thieves and thugs fall out and fight there's
     fell arrears to pay;
And soon or late sin meets its fate, and so it fell
     one day
That Claw-fingered Kitty and Windy Ike fanged
     up like dogs at bay.

"The skin is mine, all mine," she cried; "I did
     the deed alone."
"It's share and share with a guilt-yoked pair,"
     he hissed in a pregnant tone;
And so they snarled like malamutes over a mil-
     dewed bone.

And so they fought, by fear untaught, till haply
     it befell,
One dawn of day she slipped away to Dawson
     town to sell
The fruit of sin, this black fox skin that had
     made their lives a hell.

She slipped away as still he lay; she clutched
     the wondrous fur;
Her pulses beat, her foot was fleet, her fear was
     as a spur;
She laughed with glee, she did not see him rise
     and follow her.

The Ballad of the Black Fox Skin

The bluffs uprear and grimly peer far over Dawson town;
They see its lights a blaze o' nights and harshly they look down;
They mock the plan and plot of man with grim, ironic frown.

The trail was steep; 'twas at the time when swiftly sinks the snow;
All honey-combed, the river ice was rotting down below;
The river chafed beneath its rind with many a mighty throe.

And up the swift and oozy drift a woman climbed in fear,
Clutching to her a black fox fur as if she held it dear;
And hard she pressed it to her breast—then Windy Ike drew near.

She made no moan—her heart was stone—she read his smiling face,
And like a dream flashed all her life's dark horror and disgrace;
A moment only—with a snarl he hurled her into space.

She rolled for nigh an hundred feet; she bounded
    like a ball;
From crag to crag she carromed down through
    snow and timber fall. . . .
A hole gaped in the river ice; the spray flashed—
    that was all.

A bird sang for the joy of spring, so piercing
    sweet and frail;
And blinding bright the land was dight in gay
    and glittering mail;
And with a wondrous black fox skin a man slid
    down the trail.

IV.

A wedge-faced man there was who ran along the
    river bank;
Who stumbled through each drift and slough,
    and ever slipped and sank;
And ever cursed his Maker's name, and ever
    " hooch " he drank.

He travelled like a hunted thing, hard harried,
    sore distrest;
The old grandmother moon crept out from her
    cloud-quilted nest;
The aged mountains mocked at him in their
    primeval rest.

The Ballad of the Black Fox Skin

Grim shadows diapered the snow; the air was
    strangely mild;
The valley's girth was dumb with mirth, the
    laughter of the wild;
The still, sardonic laughter of an ogre o'er a
    child.

The river writhed beneath the ice; it groaned
    like one in pain,
And yawning chasms opened wide, and closed
    and yawned again;
And sheets of silver heaved on high until they
    split in twain.

From out the road-house by the trail they saw a
    man afar
Make for the narrow river-reach where the swift
    cross-currents are;
Where, frail and worn, the ice is torn and the
    angry waters jar.

But they did not see him crash and sink into the
    icy flow;
They did not see him clinging there, gripped by
    the undertow,
Clawing with bleeding finger-nails at the jagged
    ice and snow.

They found a note beside the hole where he had
 stumbled in:
"Here met his fate by evil luck a man who lived
 in sin,
And to the one who loves me least I leave this
 black fox skin."

And strange it is; for, though they searched the
 river all around,
No trace or sign of black fox skin was ever after
 found;
Though one man said he saw the tread of *hoofs*
 deep in the ground.

The vastitudes where the world protrudes through clouds like seas up-shoaled.

—Page 35

No trace or sign of black fox skin was ever after
    found;
Though one man said he saw the tread of *hoofs*
    deep in the ground.

The vastitudes where the world protrudes through
    clouds like seas up-shoaled.

The Ballad of Pious Pete

"The North has got him."—*Yukonism.*

I TRIED to refine that neighbor of mine, honest to God, I did.
I grieved for his fate, and early and late I watched over him like a kid.
I gave him excuse, I bore his abuse in every way that I could;
I swore to prevail; I camped on his trail; I plotted and planned for his good.
By day and by night I strove in men's sight to gather him into the fold,
With precept and prayer, with hope and despair, in hunger and hardship and cold.
I followed him into Gehennas of sin, I sat where the sirens sit;
In the shade of the Pole, for the sake of his soul, I strove with the powers of the Pit.

The Ballad of Pious Pete

I shadowed him down to the scrofulous town; I
    dragged him from dissolute brawls;
But I killed the galoot when he started to shoot
    electricity into my walls.

God knows what I did he should seek to be rid of
    one who would save him from shame.
God knows what I bore that night when he swore
    and bade me make tracks from his claim.
I started to tell of the horrors of hell, when sudden his eyes lit like coals;
And "Chuck it," says he, "don't persecute me
    with your cant and your saving of souls."
I'll swear I was mild as I'd be with a child, but
    he called me the son of a slut;
And, grabbing his gun with a leap and a run, he
    threatened my face with the butt.
So what could I do (I leave it to you)? With
    curses he harried me forth;
Then he was alone, and I was alone, and over us
    menaced the North.

Our cabins were near; I could see, I could hear;
    but between us there rippled the creek;
And all summer through, with a rancor that
    grew, he would pass me and never would
    speak.

Then a shuddery breath like the coming of Death
    crept down from the peaks far away;
The water was still; the twilight was chill; the
    sky was a tatter of gray.
Swift came the Big Cold, and opal and gold the
    lights of the witches arose;
The frost-tyrant clinched, and the valley was
    cinched by the stark and cadaverous
    snows.
The trees were like lace where the star-beams
    could chase, each leaf was a jewel agleam.
The soft white hush lapped the Northland and
    wrapped us round in a crystalline dream;
So still I could hear quite loud in my ear the
    swish of the pinions of time;
So bright I could see, as plain as could be, the
    wings of God's angels ashine.

As I read in the Book I would oftentimes look
    to that cabin just over the creek.
Ah me, it was sad and evil and bad, two neigh-
    bors who never would speak!
I knew that full well like a devil in hell he was
    hatching out, early and late,
A system to bear through the frost-spangled air
    the warm, crimson waves of his hate.

The Ballad of Pious Pete

I only could peer and shudder and fear—'twas
    ever so ghastly and still;
But I knew over there in his lonely despair he
    was plotting me terrible ill.
I knew that he nursed a malice accurst, like the
    blast of a winnowing flame;
I pleaded aloud for a shield, for a shroud—Oh,
    God! then calamity came.

Mad! If I'm mad then you too are mad; but it's
    all in the point of view.
If you'd looked at them things gallivantin' on
    wings, all purple and green and blue;
If you'd noticed them twist, as they mounted
    and hissed like scorpions dim in the dark;
If you'd seen them rebound with a horrible
    sound, and spitefully spitting a spark;
If you'd watched *It* with dread, as it hissed by
    your bed, that thing with the feelers that
    crawls—
You'd have settled the brute that attempted to
    shoot electricity into your walls.

Oh, some they were blue, and they slithered right
    through; they were silent and squashy and
    round;

The Ballad of Pious Pete

And some they were green; they were wriggly
 and lean; they writhed with so hateful a
 sound
My blood seemed to freeze; I fell on my knees;
 my face was a white splash of dread;
Oh, the green and the blue, they were gruesome
 to view; but the worst of them all were
 the red.
They came through the door, they came through
 the floor, they came through the moss-
 creviced logs.
They were savage and dire; they were whiskered
 with fire; they bickered like malamute
 dogs.
They ravined in rings like iniquitous things; they
 gulped down the green and the blue.
I crinkled with fear whene'er they drew near,
 and nearer and nearer they drew.

And then came the crown of Horror's grim
 crown, the monster so loathsomely red.
Each eye was a pin that shot out and in, as,
 squidlike, it oozed to my bed;
So softly it crept with feelers that swept and
 quivered like fine copper wire;
Its belly was white with a sulphurous light, its
 jaws were a-drooling with fire.

It came and it came; I could breathe of its flame,
    but never a wink could I look.
I thrust in its maw the Fount of the Law; I
    fended it off with the Book.
I was weak—oh, so weak—but I thrilled at its
    shriek, as wildly it fled in the night;
And deathlike I lay till the dawn of the day.
    (Was ever so welcome the light?)

I loaded my gun at the rise of the sun; to his
    cabin so softly I slunk.
My neighbor was there in the frost-freighted air,
    all wrapped in a robe in his bunk.
It muffled his moans; it outlined his bones, as
    feebly he twisted about;
His gums were so black, and his lips seemed to
    crack, and his teeth all were loosening out.
'Twas a death's head that peered through the
    tangle of beard; 'twas a face I will never
    forget;
Sunk eyes full of woe, and they troubled me so
    with their pleading and anguish, and yet
As I rested my gaze in a misty amaze on the
    scurvy-degenerate wreck,
I thought of the things with the dragon-fly
    wings—then laid I my gun on his neck.

He gave out a cry that was faint as a sigh, like
    a perishing malamute,
And he says unto me, "I'm converted," says he;
    " for Christ's sake, Peter, don't shoot!"

* * * * * * *

They're taking me out with an escort about, and
    under a sergeant's care;
I am humbled indeed, for I'm 'cuffed to a Swede
    that thinks he's a millionaire.
But it's all Gospel true what I'm telling to you—
    up there where the Shadow falls,
That I settled Sam Noot when he started to
    shoot electricity into my walls.

The Ballad of Blasphemous Bill

I took a contract to bury the body of blasphemous Bill MacKie,
Whenever, wherever or whatsoever the manner of death he die—
Whether he die in the light o' day or under the peak-faced moon;
In cabin or dance-hall, camp or dive, mucklucks or patent shoon;
On velvet tundra or virgin peak, by glacier, drift or draw;
In muskeg hollow or canyon gloom, by avalanche, fang or claw;
By battle, murder or sudden wealth, by pestilence, "hooch" or lead—
I swore on the Book I would follow and look till I found my tombless dead.

The Ballad of Blasphemous Bill

For Bill was a dainty kind of cuss, and his mind was mighty sot
On a dinky patch with flowers and grass in a civilized bone-yard lot.
And where he died or how he died, it didn't matter a damn
So long as he had a grave with frills, and a tombstone " epigram."
So I promised him, and he paid the price in good cheechako coin
(Which the same I blowed in that very night down in the Tenderloin).
Then I painted a three-foot slab of pine: " Here lies poor Bill MacKie,"
And I hung it up on my cabin wall and I waited for Bill to die.

Years passed away, and at last one day came a squaw with a story strange,
Of a long-deserted line of traps 'way back of the Bighorn range;
Of a little hut by the great divide, and a white man stiff and still,
Lying there by his lonesome self, and I figured it must be Bill.

So I thought of the contract I'd made with him,
    and I took down from the shelf
The swell black box with the silver plate he'd
    picked out for hisself;
And I packed it full of grub and "hooch," and
    I slung it on the sleigh;
Then I harnessed up my team of dogs and was
    off at dawn of day.

You know what it's like in the Yukon wild when
    it's sixty-nine below;
When the ice-worms wriggle their purple heads
    through the crust of the pale blue snow;
When the pine-trees crack like little guns in the
    silence of the wood,
And the icicles hang down like tusks under the
    parka hood;
When the stovepipe smoke breaks sudden off,
    and the sky is weirdly lit,
And the careless feel of a bit of steel burns like
    a red-hot spit;
When the mercury is a frozen ball, and the frost-
    fiend stalks to kill—
Well, it was just like that that day when I set
    out to look for Bill.

Oh, the awful hush that seemed to crush me
    down on every hand,
As I blundered blind with a trail to find through
    that blank and bitter land;
Half dazed, half crazed in the winter wild, with
    its grim, heart-breaking woes,
And the ruthless strife for a grip on life that
    only the sourdough knows!
North by the compass, North I pressed; river
    and peak and plain
Passed like a dream I slept to lose, and I waked
    to dream again.
River and plain and mighty peak—and who
    could stand unawed
As their summits blazed, he could stand undazed
    at the foot of the throne of God.
North, aye, North, through a land accurst,
    shunned by the scouring brutes,
And all I heard was my own harsh word and
    the whine of the malamutes,
Till at last I came to a cabin squat, built in the
    side of a hill,
And I burst in the door, and there on the floor,
    frozen to death, lay Bill.

Ice, white ice, like a winding-sheet, sheathing
    each smoke-grimed wall;

Ice on the stove-pipe, ice on the bed, ice gleam‑
   ing over all;
Sparkling ice on the dead man's chest, glittering
   ice in his hair,
Ice on his fingers, ice in his heart, ice in his
   glassy stare;
Hard as a log and trussed like a frog, with his
   arms and legs outspread.
I gazed at the coffin I'd brought for him, and I
   gazed at the gruesome dead,
And at last I spoke: "Bill liked his joke; but
   still, goldarn his eyes,
A man had ought to consider his mates in the
   way he goes and dies."

Have you ever stood in an Arctic hut in the
   shadow of the Pole,
With a little coffin six by three and a grief you
   can't control?
Have you ever sat by a frozen corpse that looks
   at you with a grin,
And that seems to say: "You may try all day,
   but you'll never jam me in"?
I'm not a man of the quitting kind, but I never
   felt so blue
As I sat there gazing at that stiff and studying
   what I'd do.

Then I rose and I kicked off the husky dogs that were nosing round about,
And I lit a roaring fire in the stove, and I started to thaw Bill out.

Well, I thawed and thawed for thirteen days, but it didn't seem no good;
His arms and legs stuck out like pegs, as if they was made of wood.
Till at last I said: "It ain't no use—he's froze too hard to thaw;
He's obstinate, and he won't lie straight, so I guess I got to—*saw*."
So I sawed off poor Bill's arms and legs, and I laid him snug and straight
In the little coffin he picked hisself, with the dinky silver plate;
And I came nigh near to shedding a tear as I nailed him safely down;
Then I stowed him away in my Yukon sleigh, and I started back to town.

So I buried him, as the contract was, in a narrow grave and deep,
And there he's waiting the Great Clean-up, when the Judgment sluice-heads sweep;

And I smoke my pipe and I meditate in the light
    of the Midnight Sun,
And sometimes I wonder if they *was*, the awful
    things I done.
And as I sit and the parson talks, expounding
    of the Law,
I often think of poor old Bill—*and how hard he
    was to saw.*

For once you've panned the speckled sand
and seen the bonny dust.

—Page 96

The Ballad of One-Eyed Mike

*THIS is the tale that was told to me by the man
  with the crystal eye,
As I smoked my pipe in the camp-fire light and
  the Glories swept the sky;
As the Northlights gleamed and curved and
  streamed, and the bottle of " hooch " was
  dry.*

A man once aimed that my life be shamed, and
  wrought me a deathly wrong;
I vowed one day I would well repay, but the heft
  of his hate was strong.
He thonged me East and he thonged me West;
  he harried me back and forth,
Till I fled in fright from his peerless spite to the
  bleak, bald-headed North.

And there I lay, and for many a day I hatched
 plan after plan
For a golden haul of the wherewithal to crush
 and to kill my man;
And there I strove, and there I clove through the
 drift of icy streams;
And there I fought, and there I sought for the
 pay-streak of my dreams.

So twenty years, with their hopes and fears
 and smiles and tears and such,
Went by and left me long bereft of hope of the
 Midas touch;
About as fat as a chancel rat, and lo! despite my
 will,
In the weary fight I had clean lost sight of the
 man I sought to kill.

'Twas so far away, that evil day when I prayed
 the Prince of Gloom
For the savage strength and the sullen length of
 life to work his doom.
Nor sign nor word had I seen or heard, and it
 happed so long ago;
My youth was gone and my memory wan, and I
 willed it even so.

The Ballad of One-Eyed Mike

It fell one night in the waning light by the
    Yukon's oily flow,
I smoked and sat as I marvelled at the sky's
    port-winey glow;
Till it paled away to an absinthe gray, and the
    river seemed to shrink,
All wobbly flakes and wriggling snakes and
    goblin eyes a-wink.

'Twas weird to see and it 'wildered me in a queer,
    hypnotic dream,
Till I saw a spot like an inky blot come floating
    down the stream;
It bobbed and swung; it sheered and hung; it
    romped round in a ring;
It seemed to play in a tricksome way; it sure was
    a merry thing.

In freakish flights strange oily lights came fluttering round its head,
Like butterflies of a monster size—then I knew
    it for the Dead.
Its face was rubbed and slicked and scrubbed as
    smooth as a shaven pate;
In the silver snakes that the water makes it
    gleamed like a dinner-plate.

It gurgled near, and clear and clear and large
 and large it grew;
It stood upright in a ring of light and it looked
 me through and through.
It weltered round with a woozy sound, and ere
 I could retreat,
With the witless roll of a sodden soul it wan-
 toned to my feet.

And here I swear by this Cross I wear, I heard
 that " floater " say:
" I am the man from whom you ran, the man
 you sought to slay.
That you may note and gaze and gloat, and say
 ' Revenge is sweet,'
In the grit and grime of the river's slime I am
 rotting at your feet.

" The ill we rue we must e'en undo, though it
 rive us bone from bone;
So it came about that I sought you out, for I
 prayed I might atone.
I did you wrong, and for long and long I sought
 where you might live;
And now you're found, though I'm dead and
 drowned, I beg you to forgive."

So sad it seemed, and its cheek-bones gleamed,
 and its fingers flicked the shore;
And it lapped and lay in a weary way, and its
 hands met to implore;
That I gently said: "Poor, restless dead, I
 would never work you woe;
Though the wrong you rue you can ne'er undo,
 I forgave you long ago."

Then, wonder-wise, I rubbed my eyes and I woke
 from a horrid dream.
The moon rode high in the naked sky, and something bobbed in the stream.
It held my sight in a patch of light, and then it
 sheered from the shore;
It dipped and sank by a hollow bank, and I
 never saw it more.

*This was the tale he told to me, that man so
 warped and gray,
Ere he slept and dreamed; and the camp-fire
 gleamed in his eye in a wolfish way—
That crystal eye that raked the sky in the weird
 Auroral ray.*

The Ballad of the Brand

'Twas up in a land long famed for gold, where
    women were far and rare,
Tellus, the smith, had taken to wife a maiden
    amazingly fair;
Tellus, the brawny worker in iron, hairy and
    heavy of hand,
Saw her and loved her and bore her away from
    the tribe of a Southern land;
Deeming her worthy to queen his home and
    mother him little ones,
That the name of Tellus, the master smith,
    might live in his stalwart sons.

Now there was little of law in the land, and evil
    doings were rife,
And every man who joyed in his home guarded
    the fame of his wife;
For there were those of the silver tongue and the
    honeyed art to beguile,

The Ballad of the Brand

Who would cozen the heart from a woman's
    breast and damn her soul with a smile.
And there were women too quick to heed a look
    or a whispered word,
And once in a while a man was slain, and the ire
    of the King was stirred;
So far and wide he proclaimed his wrath, and
    this was the Law he willed:
"That whosoever killeth a man, even shall he be
    killed."

Now Tellus, the smith, he trusted his wife; his
    heart was empty of fear.
High on the hill was the gleam of their hearth,
    a beacon of love and cheer.
High on the hill they builded their bower, where
    the broom and the bracken meet;
Under a grove of oaks it was, hushed and
    drowsily sweet.
Here he enshrined her, his dearest saint, his idol,
    the light of his eye;
Her kisses rested upon his lips as brushes a but-
    terfly.
The weight of her arms around his neck was
    light as the thistledown;
And sweetly she studied to win his smile, and
    gently she mocked his frown.

And when at the close of the dusty day his
    clangorous toil was done,
She hastened to meet him down the way all lit
    by the amber sun.
Their dove-cot gleamed in the golden light, a
    temple of stainless love;
Like the hanging cup of a big blue flower was
    the topaz sky above.
The roses and lilies yearned to her, as swift
    through their throng she pressed,
A little white, fragile, fluttering thing that lay
    like a child on his breast.
Then the heart of Tellus, the smith, was proud,
    and sang for the joy of life,
And there in the bronzing summertide he
    thanked the gods for his wife.

Now there was one called Philo, a scribe, a man
    of exquisite grace,
Carved like the god Apollo in limb, fair as
    Adonis in face;
Eager and winning of manner, full of such
    radiant charm,
Womenkind fought for his favor and loved to
    their uttermost harm.
Such was his craft and his knowledge, such was
    his skill at the game.

Never was woman could flout him, so be he
 plotted her shame.
And so he drank deep of pleasure, and then it
 fell on a day
He gazed on the wife of Tellus and marked her
 out for his prey.

Tellus, the smith, was merry, and the time of
 the year it was June,
So he said to his stalwart helpers: "Shut down
 the forge at noon.
Go ye and joy in the sunshine, rest in the coolth
 of the grove,
Drift on the dreamy river, every man with his
 love."
Then to himself: "Oh, Beloved, sweet will be
 your surprise;
To-day will we sport like children, laugh in each
 other's eyes;
Weave gay garlands of poppies, crown each
 other with flowers;
Pull plump carp from the lilies, rifle the ferny
 bowers.
To-day with feasting and gladness the wine of
 Cyprus will flow;
To-day is the day we were wedded only a twelve-
 month ago."

The larks trilled high in the heavens; **his heart**
    was lyric with joy;
He plucked a posy of lilies; he sped like a love-
    sick boy.
He stole up the velvety pathway—his cottage
    was sunsteeped and still;
Vines honeysuckled the window; **softly he**
    peeped o'er the sill.
The lilies dropped from his fingers; devils were
    choking his breath;
Rigid with horror, he stiffened; ghastly his face
    was as death.
Like a nun whose faith in the Virgin is met with
    a prurient jibe,
He shrank—'twas the wife of his bosom in the
    arms of Philo, the scribe!

Tellus went back to his smithy; he reeled like a
    drunken man;
His heart was riven with anguish; his brain was
    brooding a plan.
Straight to his anvil he hurried; started his
    furnace aglow;
Heated his iron and shaped it with savage and
    masterful blow.

The Ballad of the Brand

Sparks showered over and round him; swiftly under his hand
There at last it was finished—a hideous and infamous Brand.

That night the wife of his bosom, the light of joy in her eyes,
Kissed him with words of rapture; but he knew that her words were lies.
Never was she so beguiling, never so merry of speech
(For passion ripens a woman as the sunshine ripens a peach).
He clenched his teeth into silence; he yielded up to her lure,
Though he knew that her breasts were heaving from the fire of her paramour.
"To-morrow," he said, "to-morrow"—he wove her hair in a strand,
Twisted it round his fingers and smiled as he thought of the Brand.

The morrow was come, and Tellus swiftly stole up the hill.
Butterflies drowsed in the noon-heat; coverts were sunsteeped and still.
Softly he padded the pathway unto the porch, and within

Heard he the low laugh of dalliance, heard he
    the rapture of sin.
Knew he her eyes were mystic with light that no
    man should see,
No man kindle and joy in, no man on earth save
    he.
And never for him would it kindle. The blood-
    lust surged in his brain;
Through the senseless stone could he see them,
    wanton and warily fain.
Horrible! Heaven he sought for, gained it and
    gloried and fell—
Oh, it was sudden—headlong into the nether-
    most hell. . . .

Was this he, Tellus, this marble? Tellus . . .
    not dreaming a dream?
Ah! sharp-edged as a javelin, was that a woman's
    scream?
Was it a door that shattered, shell-like, under
    his blow?
Was it his saint, that strumpet, dishevelled and
    cowering low?
Was it her lover, that wild thing, that twisted
    and gouged and tore?
Was it a man he was crushing, whose head he
    beat on the floor?

Laughing the while at its weakness, till sudden he stayed his hand—
Through the red ring of his madness flamed the thought of the Brand.

Then bound he the naked Philo with thongs that cut in the flesh,
And the wife of his bosom, fear-frantic, he gagged with a silken mesh,
Choking her screams into silence; bound her down by the hair;
Dragged her lover unto her under her frenzied stare.
In the heat of the hearth-fire embers he heated the hideous Brand;
Twisting her fingers open, he forced its haft in her hand.
He pressed it downward and downward; she felt the living flesh sear;
She saw the throe of her lover; she heard the scream of his fear.
Once, twice and thrice he forced her, heedless of prayer and shriek—
Once on the forehead of Philo, twice in the soft of his cheek.
Then (for the thing was finished) he said to the woman: "See

How you have branded your lover! Now will I
    let him go free."
He severed the thongs that bound him, laughing:
    " Revenge is sweet,"
And Philo, sobbing in anguish, feebly rose to his
    feet.
The man who was fair as Apollo, god-like in
    woman's sight,
Hideous now as a satyr, fled to the pity of night.

*Then came they before the Judgment Seat, and
    thus spoke the Lord of the Land:*
*" He who seeketh his neighbor's wife shall suffer
    the doom of the Brand.*
*Brutish and bold on his brow be it stamped, deep
    in his cheek let it sear,*
*That every man may look on his shame, and
    shudder and sicken and fear.*
*He shall hear their mock in the market-place,
    their fleering jibe at the feast;*
*He shall seek the caves and the shroud of night,
    and the fellowship of the beast.*
*Outcast forever from homes of men, far and far
    shall he roam.*
*Such be the doom, sadder than death, of him who
    shameth a home."*

The big, blue, silt-freighted Yukon.
—Page 110

The Ballad of the Brand

"I have branded your lover! Now will I
    let him go free."
Cut the thongs that bound him, laughing:
    "Revenge is sweet."
And he, sobbing in anguish, feebly rose to his
    feet.
The man who was fair as Apollo, god-like in
    woman's sight,
Hideous now as a satyr, fled to the pity of night.

Then came they before the Judgment Seat, and
    thus spoke the Lord of the Land:
"He who seeketh his neighbor's wife shall suffer
    the doom of the Brand.
Brutish and bold on his brow be it stamped, deep
    in his cheek let it sear;
That every man may look on his shame, and
    shudder and sicken and fear.
Fear their mock in the market-place,
    their leering jibe at the feast;
He shall seek the caves and the shroud of night,
    and the fellowship of the beast.

The Ballad of Hard-Luck Henry

Now wouldn't you expect to find a man an awful
    crank
That's staked out nigh three hundred claims,
    and every one a blank;
That's followed every fool stampede, and seen
    the rise and fall
Of camps where men got gold in chunks and he
    got none at all;
That's prospected a bit of ground and sold it for
    a song,
To see it yield a fortune to some fool that came
    along;
That's sunk a dozen bed-rock holes, and not a
    speck in sight,
Yet sees them take a million from the claims to
    left and right.
Now aren't things like that enough to drive a
    man to booze?
But Hard-Luck Smith was hoodoo-proof—he
    knew the way to lose.

'Twas in the fall of nineteen four—leap-year, I've heard them say—
When Hard-Luck came to Hunker Creek and took a hillside lay.
And lo! as if to make amends for all the futile past,
Late in the year he struck it rich, the real pay-streak at last.
The riffles of his sluicing-box were choked with speckled earth,
And night and day he worked that lay for all that he was worth.
And when in chill December's gloom his lucky lease expired,
He found that he had made a stake as big as he desired.

One day while meditating on the waywardness of fate,
He felt the ache of lonely man to find a fitting mate;
A petticoated pard to cheer his solitary life,
A woman with soft, soothing ways, a confidant, a wife.
And, while he cooked his supper on his little Yukon stove,

The Ballad of Hard-Luck Henry

He wished that he had staked a claim in Love's
  rich treasure-trove;
And suddenly he paused and held aloft a Yukon
  egg,
For there in penciled letters was the magic name
  of Peg.

You know these Yukon eggs of ours—some pink,
  some green, some blue—
A dollar per, assorted tints, assorted flavors too.
The supercilious cheechako might designate them
  high,
But one acquires a taste for them and likes them
  by-and-by.
Well, Hard-Luck Henry took this egg and held
  it to the light,
And there was more faint penciling that sorely
  taxed his sight.
At last he made it out, and then the legend ran
  like this—
"Will Klondike miner write to Peg, Plumhol-
  low, Squashville, Wis.?"

That night he got to thinking of this far-off, unknown fair;
It seemed so sort of opportune, an answer to his
  prayer.

The Ballad of Hard-Luck Henry

She flitted sweetly through his dreams, she haunted him by day,
She smiled through clouds of nicotine, she cheered his weary way.
At last he yielded to the spell; his course of love he set—
Wisconsin his objective point; his object, Margaret.

With every mile of sea and land his longing grew and grew.
He practised all his pretty words, and these, I fear, were few.
At last, one frosty evening, with a cold chill down his spine,
He found himself before her house, the threshold of the shrine.
His courage flickered to a spark, then glowed with sudden flame—
He knocked, he heard a welcome word; she came —his goddess came.
Oh, she was fair as any flower, and huskily he spoke:
"I'm all the way from Klondike, with a mighty heavy poke.

The Ballad of Hard-Luck Henry

I'm looking for a lassie, one whose Christian
    name is Peg,
Who sought a Klondike miner, and who wrote it
    on an egg."

The lassie gazed at him a space, her cheeks grew
    rosy red;
She gazed at him with tear-bright eyes, then ten-
    derly she said:
"Yes, lonely Klondike miner, it is true my name
    is Peg.
It's also true I longed for you and wrote it on an
    egg.
My heart went out to someone in that land of
    night and cold;
But oh, I fear that Yukon egg must have been
    mighty old.
I waited long, I hoped and feared; you should
    have come before;
I've been a wedded woman now for eighteen
    months or more.
I'm sorry, since you've come so far, you ain't the
    one that wins;
But won't you take a step inside—*I'll let you
    see the twins.*"

The Ballad of Gum-Boot Ben

*HE was an old prospector with a vision bleared
    and dim.*
*He asked me for a grubstake, and the same 1
    gave to him.*
*He hinted of a hidden trove, and when I made
    so bold*
To question his veracity, this is the tale he told:

"I do not seek the copper streak, nor yet the yel-
    low dust;
I am not fain for sake of gain to irk the frozen
    crust;
Let fellows gross find gilded dross, far other is
    my mark;
Oh, gentle youth, this is the truth—I go to seek
    the Ark.

There was the rage of the rapids.
—Page 125

Ballad of Gum-Boot Ben

He was an old prospector with a vision bleared and dim.
He asked me for a grubstake, and the same I gave to him.
He hinted of a hidden trove, and when I made so bold
To question his veracity, this is the tale he told:

"I prospected the Pelly bed, I prospected the White;
The Nordenscold for love of gold I piked from morn till night;
Afar and near for many a year I led the wild stampede,
Until I guessed that all my quest was vanity and greed.

"Then came I to a land I knew no man had ever been;
A haggard land forlornly spanned by mountains lank and lean.
The nitches said 'twas full of dread, of smoke and fiery breath,
And no man dare put foot in there for fear of pain and death.

"But I was made all unafraid, so, careless and alone,
Day after day I made my way into that land unknown;
Night after night by camp-fire light I crouched in lonely thought;
Oh, gentle youth, this is the truth—I knew not what I sought.

The Ballad of Gum-Boot Ben

" I rose at dawn; I wandered on; 'tis somewhat
 fine and grand
To be alone and hold your own in God's vast
 awesome land;
Come woe or weal, 'tis fine to feel a hundred
 miles between
The trails you dare and pathways where the feet
 of men have been.

" And so it fell on me a spell of wander-lust was
 cast.
The land was still and strange and chill, and
 cavernous and vast;
And sad and dead, and dull as lead the valleys
 sought the snows;
And far and wide on every side the ashen peaks
 arose.

" The moon was like a silent spike that pierced
 the sky right through;
The small stars popped and winked and hopped
 in vastitudes of blue;
And unto me for company came creatures of the
 shade,
And formed in rings and whispered things that
 made me half afraid.

"And strange though be, 'twas borne in me that
    land had lived of old;
And men had crept and slain and slept where
    now they toiled for gold;
Through jungles dim the mammoth grim had
    sought the oozy fen,
And on his track, all bent of back, had crawled
    the hairy men.

"And furthermore strange deeds of yore in this
    dead place were done.
They haunted me, as wild and free I roamed
    from sun to sun;
Until I came where sudden flame uplit a terraced
    height,
A regnant peak that seemed to seek the coronal
    of night.

"I scaled the peak; my heart was weak, yet on
    and on I pressed.
Skyward I strained until I gained its dazzling
    silver crest,
And there I found, with all around a world
    supine and stark,
Swept clean of snow, a flat plateau, and on it
    lay—the Ark.

"Yes, there I knew by two and two the beasts
     did disembark,
And so in haste I ran and traced in letters on
     the Ark
My human name, Ben Smith's the same; and
     now I want to float
A syndicate to haul and freight to town that
     noble boat."

I met him later in a bar and made a gay remark
Anent an ancient miner and an option on the
     Ark.
He gazed at me reproachfully, as only topers can;
But what he said I can't repeat—he was a bad
     old man.

The Man from Eldorado

I.

He's the man from Eldorado, and he's just arrived in town,
  In moccasins and oily buckskin shirt.
He's gaunt as any Indian, and pretty nigh as brown;
  He's greasy, and he smells of sweat and dirt.
He sports a crop of whiskers that would shame a healthy hog;
  Hard work has racked his joints and stooped his back;
He slops along the sidewalk followed by his yellow dog,
  But he's got a bunch of gold-dust in his sack.

He seems a little wistful as he blinks at all the lights,
  And maybe he is thinking of his claim
And the dark and dwarfish cabin where he lay and dreamed at nights,

(Thank God, he'll never see the place again!)
Where he lived on tinned tomatoes, beef em-
    balmed and sourdough bread,
  On rusty beans and bacon furred with mould.
His stomach's out of kilter and his system full
    of lead,
  But it's over, and his poke is full of gold.

He has panted at the windlass, he has loaded in
    the drift,
  He has pounded at the face of oozy clay;
He has taxed himself to sickness, dark and damp
    and double shift,
  He has labored like a demon night and day.
And now, praise God, it's over, and he seems to
    breathe again
  The new-mown hay, the warm, wet, friendly
    loam;
He sees a snowy orchard in a green and dimp-
    ling plain,
  And a little vine-clad cottage, and it's—Home.

II.

He's the man from Eldorado, and he's had a bite
    and sup,
  And he's met in with a drouthy friend or two;

He's cached away his gold-dust, but he's sort of
    bucking up,
  So he's kept enough to-night to see him
    through.
His eye is bright and genial, his tongue no longer
    lags;
  His heart is brimming o'er with joy and mirth;
He may be far from savory, he may be clad in
    rags,
  But to-night he feels as if he owns the earth.

Says he: "Boys, here is where the shaggy North
    and I will shake;
  I thought I'd never manage to get free.
I kept on making misses; but at last I've got my
    stake;
  There's no more thawing frozen muck for me.
I am going to God's Country, where I'll live the
    simple life;
  I'll buy a bit of land and make a start;
I'll carve a little homestead, and I'll win a little
    wife,
  And raise ten little kids to cheer my heart."

  They signified their sympathy by crowding to
    the bar;

They bellied up three deep and drank his
  health.
He shed a radiant smile around and smoked a
  rank cigar;
They wished him honor, happiness and wealth.
They drank unto his wife to be—that unsuspect-
  ing maid;
They drank unto his children half a score;
And when they got through drinking, very ten-
  derly they laid
The man from Eldorado on the floor.

III.

He's the man from Eldorado, and he's only start-
  ing in
  To cultivate a thousand-dollar jag.
His poke is full of gold-dust and his heart is full
  of sin,
  And he's dancing with a girl called Mucluc
    Mag.
She's as light as any fairy; she's as pretty as a
  peach;
  She's mistress of the witchcraft to beguile;
There's sunshine in her manner, there is music
  in her speech,
  And there's concentrated honey in her smile.

Oh, the fever of the dance-hall and the glitter and
 the shine,
The beauty, and the jewels, and the whirl,
The madness of the music, the rapture of the
 wine,
The languorous allurement of a girl!
She is like a lost madonna; he is gaunt, unkempt
 and grim;
But she fondles him and gazes in his eyes;
Her kisses seek his heavy lips, and soon it seems
 to him
He has staked a little claim in Paradise.

"Who's for a juicy two-step?" cries the master
 of the floor;
The music throbs with soft, seductive beat.
There's glitter, gilt and gladness; there are
 pretty girls galore;
There's a woolly man with moccasins on feet.
They know they've got him going; he is buying
 wine for all;
They crowd around as buzzards at a feast;
Then when his poke is empty they boost him
 from the hall,
And spurn him in the gutter like a beast.

He's the man from Eldorado, and he's painting
    red the town;
  Behind he leaves a trail of yellow dust;
In a whirl of senseless riot he is ramping up and
    down;
  There's nothing checks his madness and his
    lust.
And soon the word is passed around—it travels
    like a flame;
  They fight to clutch his hand and call him
    friend,
The chevaliers of lost repute, the dames of sorry
    fame;
  Then comes the grim awakening—the end.

IV.

He's the man from Eldorado, and he gives a
    grand affair;
  There's feasting, dancing, wine without re-
    straint.
The smooth Beau Brummels of the bar, the faro
    men, are there;
  The tinhorns and purveyors of red paint;
The sleek and painted women, their predacious
    eyes aglow—
  Sure Klondike City never saw the like;

Then Mucluc Mag proposed the toast, "The giver
    of the show,
  The livest sport that ever hit the pike."

The "live one" rises to his feet; he stammers to
    reply—
And then there comes before his muddled brain
A vision of green vastitudes beneath an April
    sky,
  And clover pastures drenched with silver rain.
He knows that it can never be, that he is down
    and out;
  . Life leers at him with foul and fetid breath;
And then amid the revelry, the song and cheer
    and shout,
  He suddenly grows grim and cold as death.

He grips the table tensely, and he says: "Dear
    friends of mine,
  I've let you dip your fingers in my purse;
I've crammed you at my table, and I've drowned
    you in my wine,
  And I've little left to give you but—my curse.
I've failed supremely in my plans; its rather late
    to whine;
  My poke is mighty weasened up and small.

I thank you each for coming here, the happiness
  is mine—
And now, you thieves and harlots, take it all."

He twists the thong from off his poke; he swings
  it o'er his head;
The nuggets fall around their feet like grain.
They rattle over roof and wall; they scatter, roll
  and spread;
The dust is like a shower of golden rain.
The guests a moment stand aghast, then grovel
  on the floor;
They fight, and snarl, and claw, like beasts of
  prey;
And then, as everybody grabbed and everybody
  swore,
The man from Eldorado slipped away.

V.

He's the man from Eldorado, and they found
  him stiff and dead,
Half covered by the freezing ooze and dirt.
A clotted Colt was in his hand, a hole was in his
  head,
And he wore an old and oily buckskin shirt.

The Man from Eldorado

His eyes were fixed and horrible, as one who hails the end;
The frost had set him rigid as a log;
And there, half lying on his breast, his last and only friend,
There crouched and whined a mangy yellow dog.

My Friends

The man above was a murderer, the man below
 was a thief;
And I lay there in the bunk between, ailing beyond belief;
A weary armful of skin and bone, wasted with
 pain and grief.

My feet were froze, and the lifeless toes were
 purple and green and gray;
The little flesh that clung to my bones you could
 punch it in holes like clay;
The skin on my gums was a sullen black, and
 slowly peeling away.

I was sure enough in a direful fix, and often I
 wondered why
They did not take the chance that was left, and
 leave me alone to die,
Or finish me off with a dose of dope—so utterly
 lost was I.

The lonely waif of the wood-camp.
—Page 112

My Friends

...n above was a murderer, the man below
...as a thief;
...lay there in the bunk between, ailing be-
...ond belief;
...y armful of skin and bone, wasted with
...ain and grief.

...t were froze, and the lifeless toes were
...urple and green and gray;
...e flesh that clung to my bones you could
...unch it in holes like clay;
...n on my gums was a sullen black, and
...lowly peeling away.

...ure enough in a direful fix, and often I
...vondered why
...d not take the chance that was left, and
...eave me alone to die,
...h me off with a dose of dope—so utterly

But no; they brewed me the green-spruce tea,
    and nursed me there like a child;
And the homicide he was good to me, and bathed
    my sores and smiled;
And the thief he starved that I might be fed,
    and his eyes were kind and mild.

Yet they were woefully wicked men, and often
    at night in pain
I heard the murderer speak of his deed, and
    dream it over again;
I heard the poor thief sorrowing for the dead
    self he had slain.

I'll never forget that bitter dawn, so evil, askew
    and gray,
When they wrapped me round in the skins of
    beasts and they bore me to a sleigh,
And we started out with the nearest post an
    hundred miles away.

I'll never forget the trail they broke, with its
    tense, unuttered woe;
And the crunch, crunch, crunch as their snow-
    shoes sank through the crust of the hollow
    snow;
And my breath would fail, and every beat of my
    heart was like a blow.

And oftentimes I would die the death, yet wake
    up to life anew;
The sun would be all ablaze on the waste, and
    the sky a blighting blue,
And the tears would rise in my snow-blind eyes
    and furrow my cheeks like dew.

And the camps we made when their strength out-
    played, and the day was pinched and wan;
And oh, the joy of that blessed halt, and how I
    did dread the dawn;
And how I hated the weary men who rose and
    dragged me on.

And oh, how I begged to rest, to rest—the snow
    was so sweet a shroud;
And oh, how I cried when they urged me on,
    cried and cursed them aloud;
Yet on they strained, all racked and pained, and
    sorely their backs were bowed.

And then it was all like a lurid dream, and I
    prayed for a swift release
From the ruthless ones who would not leave me
    to die alone in peace;
Till I wakened up, and I found myself at the
    post of the Mounted Police.

My Friends

And there was my friend the murderer, and there was my friend the thief,
With bracelets of steel around their wrists, and wicked beyond belief:
But when they come to God's judgment seat— may I be allowed the brief.

The Prospector

I STROLLED up old Bonanza, where I staked in
    ninety-eight,
  A-purpose to revisit the old claim.
I kept thinking mighty sadly of the funny ways
    of Fate,
  And the lads who once were with me in the
    game.
Poor boys, they're down-and-outers, and there's
    scarcely one to-day
  Can show a dozen colors in his poke;
And me, I'm still prospecting, old and battered,
    gaunt and gray,
  And I'm looking for a grub-stake, and I'm
    broke.

I strolled up old Bonanza. The same old moon
    looked down;
  The same old landmarks seemed to yearn to
    me;

The Prospector

But the cabins all were silent, and the flat, once
    like a town,
Was mighty still and lonesome-like to see.
There were piles and piles of tailings where we
    toiled with pick and pan,
And turning round a bend I heard a roar;
And there a giant gold-ship of the very newest
    plan
Was tearing chunks of pay-dirt from the shore.

It wallowed in its water-bed; it burrowed, heaved
    and swung;
It gnawed its way ahead with grunt and sighs;
Its bill of fare was rock and sand; the tailings
    were its dung;
It glared around with fierce electric eyes.
Full fifty buckets crammed its maw; it bellowed
    out for more;
It looked like some great monster in the gloom.
With two to feed its sateless greed, it worked for
    seven score,
    And I sighed: " Ah, old-time miner, here's your
        doom!"

The idle windlass turns to rust; the sagging
    sluice-box falls;
The holes you digged are water to the brim;

The Prospector

Your little sod-roofed cabins with the snugly
  moss-chinked walls,
Are deathly now and mouldering and dim.
The battle-field is silent, where of old you fought
  it out;
The claims you fiercely won are lost and sold;
But there's a little army that they'll never put
  to rout—
The men who simply live to seek the gold.

The men who can't remember when they learned
  to swing a pack,
Or in what lawless land the quest began;
The solitary seeker with his grub-stake on his
  back,
The restless buccaneer of pick and pan.
On the mesas of the Southland, on the tundras
  of the North,
  You will find us, changed in face, but still
    the same;
And it isn't need, it isn't greed that sends us
  faring forth—
(It's the fever, it's the glory of the game.)

For once you've panned the speckled sand and
  seen the bonny dust,
  Its peerless brightness blinds you like a spell;

It's little else you care about; you go because
   you must,
 And you feel that you could follow it to hell.
You'd follow it in hunger, and you'd follow it in
   cold;
 You'd follow it in solitude and pain;
And when you're stiff and battened down let
   someone whisper " Gold,"
 You're lief to rise and follow it again.

Yet look you, if I find the stuff it's just like so
   much dirt;
 I fling it to the four winds like a child.
It's wine and painted women and the things that
   do me hurt,
 Till I crawl back, beggared, broken, to the
   Wild.
Till I crawl back, sapped and sodden, to my
   grub-stake and my tent;
 There's a city, there's an army (hear them
   shout).
There's the gold in millions, millions, but I
   haven't got a cent;
 And oh, it's me, it's me that found it out.

It was my dream that made it good; my dream
   that made me go
 To lands of dread and death disprized of man.

But oh, I've known a glory that their hearts will
    never know
  When I picked the first big nugget from my
    pan.
It's still my dream, my dauntless dream that
    drives me forth once more,
  To seek and starve and suffer in the Vast;
That heaps my heart with eager hope, that
    glimmers on before—
  My dream that will uplift me to the last.

Perhaps I am stark crazy, but there's none of
    you too sane;
  It's just a little matter of degree.
My hobby is to hunt out gold; it's fortressed in
    my brain;
  It's life and love and wife and home to me.
And I'll strike it, yes, I'll strike it; I've a hunch
    I cannot fail;
  I've a vision, I've a prompting, I've a call;
I hear the hoarse stampeding of an army on my
    trail,
  To the last, the greatest gold camp of them all.

Beyond the shark-tooth ranges sawing savage at
    the sky
  There's a lowering land no white man ever
    struck;

Your little tongue makes a
rush at the clumsy fly.

—Page 23

Your little sod-roofed cabins with the snugly moss-chinked walls.

Page 96

O'er soundless lakes, where the grayling makes a rush at the clumsy fly.

—Page 23

O'er soundless lakes, where the grayling makes a
rush at the clumsy fly

—Page 25

We tightened our girths and our pack-straps; we linked on the Human Chain,
Struggling up to the summit, where every step was a pain.

—Page 120

We tightened our girths and our pack-straps; we linked on the Human Chain, struggling up to the summit, where every step was a pain.

—*Page 120*

The Prospector

There's gold, there's gold in millions, and I'll
    find it if I die,
And I'm going there once more to try my luck.
Maybe I'll fail—what matter? It's a mandate,
    it's a vow;
And when in lands of dreariness and dread
You seek the last lone frontier, far beyond your
    frontiers now,
    You will find the old prospector, silent, dead.

You will find a tattered tent-pole with a ragged
    robe below it;
You will find a rusted gold-pan on the sod;
You will find the claim I'm seeking, with my
    bones as stakes to show it;
    But I've sought the last Recorder, and He's—
    God.

The Black Sheep

"The aristocratic ne'er-do-well in Canada frequently finds his way into the ranks of the Royal North-West Mounted Police."—*Extract.*

HARK to the ewe that bore him:
  "What has muddied the strain?
Never his brothers before him
  Showed the hint of a stain."
Hark to the tups and wethers;
  Hark to the old gray ram:
"We're all of us white, but he's black as night,
  And he'll never be worth a damn."

I'm up on the bally wood-pile at the back of the
    barracks yard;
"A damned disgrace to the force, sir," with a
    comrade standing guard;
Making the bluff I'm busy, doing my six months
    hard.

The Black Sheep

"Six months hard and dismissed, sir." Isn't
 that rather hell?
And all because of the liquor laws and the wiles
 of a native belle—
Some "hooch" I gave to a Siwash brave who
 swore that he wouldn't tell.

At least they *say* that I did it. It's so in the
 town report.
All that I can recall is a night of revel and sport,
When I woke with a "head" in the guard-room,
 and they dragged me sick into court.

And the O. C. said: "You are guilty," and I said
 never a word;
For, hang it, you see I couldn't—I didn't know
 what had occurred,
And, under the circumstances, denial would be
 absurd.

But the one that cooked my bacon was Grubbe
 of the City Patrol.
He fagged for my room at Eton, and didn't I
 devil his soul!
And now he is getting even, landing me down in
 the hole.

Plugging away on the wood-pile; doing chores
    round the square.
There goes an officer's lady—gives me a haughty
    stare—
Me that's an earl's own nephew—that is the
    hardest to bear.

To think of the poor old mater awaiting her
    prodigal son.
Tho' I broke her heart with my folly, I was al-
    ways the white-haired one.
(That fatted calf that they're cooking will
    surely be overdone.)

I'll go back and yarn to the Bishop; I'll dance
    with the village belle;
I'll hand round tea to the ladies and everything
    will be well.
Where I have been won't matter; what I have
    seen I won't tell.

I'll soar to their ken like a comet. They'll see
    me with never a stain;
But will they reform me?—far from it. We pay
    for our pleasure with pain;
But the dog will return to his vomit, the hog to
    his wallow again.

The Black Sheep

I've chewed on the rind of creation, and bitter
　　I've tasted the same;
Stacked up against hell and damnation, I've
　　managed to stay in the game;
I've had my moments of sorrow; I've had my
　　seasons of shame.

That's past; when one's nature's a cracked one,
　　it's too jolly hard to mend.
So long as the road is level so long as I've cash
　　to spend,
I'm bound to go to the devil, and it's all the same
　　in the end.

The bugle is sounding for stables; the men troop
　　off through the gloom;
An orderly laying the tables sings in the bright
　　mess-room.
(I'll wash in the prison bucket, and brush with
　　the prison broom.)

I'll lie in my cell and listen; I'll wish that I
　　couldn't hear
The laugh and the chaff of the fellows swigging
　　the canteen beer;
The nasal tone of the gramophone playing " The
　　Bandolier."

And it seems to me, though it's misty, that night
  of the flowing bowl,
That the man who potlatched the whiskey and
  landed me into the hole
Was Grubbe, that unmerciful bounder, Grubbe,
  of the City Patrol.

Nothing but rock and tree;
Nothing but wood and stone.
—Page 105

who potlatched the whiskey and
ne into the hole
hat unmerciful bounder, Grubbe,
'ity Patrol.

Nothing but rock and tree;
Nothing but wood and ston

The Telegraph Operator

I WILL not wash my face;
   I will not brush my hair;
I "pig" around the place—
   There's nobody to care.
Nothing but rock and tree;
   Nothing but wood and stone;
Oh God, it's hell to be
   Alone, alone, alone.

Snow-peaks and deep-gashed draws
   Corral me in a ring.
I feel as if I was
   The only living thing
On all this blighted earth;
   And so I frowst and shrink,
And crouching by my hearth,
   I hear the thoughts I think.

I think of all I miss—
　　The boys I used to know;
The girls I used to kiss;
　　The coin I used to blow;
The bars I used to haunt;
　　The racket and the row;
The beers I didn't want
　　(I wish I had 'em now).

Day after day the same,
　　Only a little worse;
No one to grouch or blame—
　　Oh, for a loving curse!
Oh, in the night I fear,
　　Haunted by nameless things,
Just for a voice to cheer,
　　Just for a hand that clings!

Faintly as from a star
　　Voices come o'er the line;
Voices of ghosts afar,
　　Not in this world of mine.
Lives in whose loom I grope;
　　Words in whose weft I hear
Eager the thrill of hope,
　　Awful the chill of fear.

The Telegraph Operator

I'm thinking out aloud;
  I reckon that is bad;
(The snow is like a shroud)—
  Maybe I'm going mad.
Say! wouldn't that be tough?
  This awful hush that hugs
And chokes one is enough
  To make a man go " bugs."

There's not a thing to do;
  I cannot sleep at night;
No wonder I'm so blue;
  Oh, for a friendly fight!
The din and rush of strife;
  A music-hall aglow;
A crowd, a city, life—
  Dear God, I miss it so!

Here, you have moped enough!
  Brace up and play the game!
But say, it's awful tough—
  Day after day the same.
(I've said that twice, I bet).
  Well, there's not much to say.
I wish I had a pet,
  Or something I could play.

The Telegraph Operator

Cheer up! don't get so glum
   And sick of everything;
The worst is yet to come;
   God help you till the Spring.
God shield you from the Fear;
   Teach you to laugh, not moan.
Ha! ha! it sounds so queer—
   Alone, alone, alone.

The Wood-Cutter.

THE sky is like an envelope,
  One of those blue official things;
And, sealing it, to mock our hope,
  The moon, a silver wafer, clings.
What shall we find when death gives leave
To read—our sentence or reprieve?

I'm holding it down on God's scrap-pile, up on
    the fag-end of earth;
  O'er me a menace of mountains, a river that
    grits at my feet;
Face to face with my soul-self, weighing my life
    at its worth;
  Wondering what I was made for, here in my
    last retreat.

Last! Ah, yes, it's the finish. Have ever you
    heard a man cry?
  (Sobs that rake him and rend him, right from
    the base of the chest.)
That's how I've cried, oh, so often; and now
    that my tears are dry,
  I sit in the desolate quiet and wait for the
    infinite Rest.

Rest! Well, it's restful around me; it's quiet
    clean to the core.
  The mountains pose in their ermine, in golden
    the hills are clad;
The big, blue, silt-freighted Yukon seethes by my
    cabin door,
  And I think it's only the river that keeps me
    from going mad.

By day it's ruthless monster, a callous, insatiate
    thing,
  With oily bubble and eddy, with sudden swirl-
    ing of breast;
By night it's a writhing Titan, sullenly murmur-
    ing,
  Ever and ever goaded, and ever crying for
    rest.

It cries for its human tribute, but me it will never drown.
 I've learned the lore of my river; my river obeys me well.
I hew and I launch my cordwood, and raft it to Dawson town,
 Where wood means wine and women, and, incidentally, hell.

Hell and anguish thereafter. Here as I sit alone
 I'd give the life I have left me to lighten some load of care.
(The bitterest part of the bitter is being denied to atone;
 Lips that have mocked at Heaven lend themselves ill to prayer.)

Impotent as a beetle pierced on the needle of Fate;
 A wretch in a cosmic death cell, peaks for my prison bars;
Whelmed by a world stupendous, lonely and listless I wait,
 Drowned in a sea of silence, strewn with confetti of stars.

The Wood-Cutter

See! from far up the valley a rapier pierces the night,
   The white search-ray of a steamer; swiftly, serenely it nears;
A proud, white, alien presence, a glittering galley of light,
   Confident-poised, triumphant, freighted with hopes and fears.

I look as one looks on a vision; I see it pulsating by;
   I glimpse joy-radiant faces; I hear the thresh of the wheel.
Hoof-like my heart beats a moment; then silence swoops from the sky;
   Darkness is piled upon darkness. God only knows how I feel.

Maybe you've seen me sometimes; maybe you've pitied me then—
   The lonely waif of the wood-camp, here by my cabin door.
Some day you'll look and see not; futile and outcast of men,
   I shall be far from your pity, resting forevermore.

*My life was a problem in ciphers, a weary and
   profitless sum.
Slipshod and stupid I worked it, dazed by
   negation and doubt.
Ciphers the total confronts me. O Death, with
   thy moistened thumb,
Stoop like a petulant schoolboy, wipe me forever out!*

The Song of the Mouth Organ

(With apologies to the singer of the "Song of the Banjo.")

I'm a homely little bit of tin and bone;
   I'm beloved by the Legion of the Lost;
I haven't got a "vox humana" tone,
   And a dime or two will satisfy my cost.
I don't attempt your high-falutin' flights;
   I am more or less uncertain on the key;
But I tell you, boys, there's lots and lots of nights
   When you've taken mighty comfort out of me.

I weigh an ounce or two, and I'm so small
   You can pack me in the pocket of your vest;
And when at night so wearily you crawl
   Into your bunk and stretch your limbs to rest.
You take me out and play me soft and low,
   The simple songs that trouble your heart-strings;
The tunes you used to fancy long ago,
   Before you made a rotten mess of things.

Then a dreamy look will come into your eyes,
  And you break off in the middle of a note;
And then, with just the dreariest of sighs,
  You drop me in the pocket of your coat.
But somehow I have bucked you up a bit;
  And, as you turn around and face the wall,
You don't feel quite so spineless and unfit—
  You're not so bad a fellow after all.

Do you recollect the bitter Arctic night;
  Your camp beside the canyon on the trail;
Your tent a tiny square of orange light;
  The moon above consumptive-like and pale;
Your supper cooked, your little stove aglow;
  You tired, but snug and happy as a child?
Then 'twas " Turkey in the Straw " till your lips
    were nearly raw,
  And you hurled your bold defiance at the Wild.

Do you recollect the flashing, lashing pain;
  The gulf of humid blackness overhead;
The lightning making rapiers of the rain;
  The cattle-horns like candles of the dead;
You sitting on your bronco there alone,
  In your slicker, saddle-sore and sick with cold?
Do you think the silent herd did not hear " The
    Mocking Bird,"
  Or relish " Silver Threads among the Gold "?

The Song of the Mouth-Organ

Do you recollect the wild Magellan coast;
    The head-winds and the icy, roaring seas;
The nights you thought that everything was lost;
    The days you toiled in water to your knees;
The frozen ratlines shrieking in the gale;
    The hissing steeps and gulfs of livid foam:
When you cheered your messmates nine with
        "Ben Bolt" and "Clementine,"
    And "Dixie Land" and "Seeing Nellie
        Home"?

Let the jammy banjo voice the Younger Son,
    Who waits for his remittance to arrive;
I represent the grimy, gritty one,
    Who sweats his bones to keep himself alive;
Who's up against the real thing from his birth;
    Whose heritage is hard and bitter toil;
I voice the weary, smeary ones of earth,
    The helots of the sea and of the soil.

I'm the Steinway of strange mischief and mischance;
    I'm the Stradivarius of blank defeat;
In the down-world, when the devil leads the dance,
    I am simply and symbolically meet;

The Song of the Mouth-Organ

I'm the irrepressive spirit of mankind;
  I'm the small boy playing knuckle-down with
    Death;
At the end of all things known, where God's
    rubbish-heap is thrown,
  I shrill impudent triumph at a breath.

I'm a humble little bit of tin and horn;
  I'm a byeword, I'm a plaything, I'm a jest;
The virtuoso looks on me with scorn;
  But there's times when I am better than the
    best.
Ask the stoker and the sailor of the sea;
  Ask the mucker and the hewer of the pine;
Ask the herder of the plain, ask the gleaner of
    the grain—
  There's a lowly, loving kingdom—and it's
    mine.

The Trail of Ninety-Eight

I.

GOLD! We leapt from our benches. Gold! We
    sprang from our stools.
Gold! We wheeled in the furrow, fired with the
    faith of fools.
Fearless, unfound, unfitted, far from the night
    and the cold,
Heard we the clarion summons, followed the
    master-lure—Gold!

Men from the sands of the Sunland; men from
    the woods of the West;
Men from the farms and the cities, into the
    Northland we pressed.
Greybeards and striplings and women, good men
    and bad men and bold,
Leaving our homes and our loved ones, crying
    exultantly—"Gold!"

Never was seen such an army, pitiful, futile, unfit;
Never was seen such a spirit, manifold courage and grit;
Never has been such a cohort under one banner enrolled,
As surged to the ragged-edged Arctic, urged by the arch-tempter—Gold.

"Farewell," we cried to our dearests; little we cared for their tears.
"Farewell," we cried to the humdrum and the yoke of the hireling years;
Just like a pack of school-boys, and the big crowd cheered us good-bye.
Never were hearts so uplifted, never were hopes so high.

The spectral shores flitted past us, and every whirl of the screw
Hurled us nearer to fortune, and ever we planned what we'd do—
Do with the gold when we got it—big, shiny nuggets like plums,
There in the sand of the river, gouging it out with our thumbs.

And one man wanted a castle, another a racing
 stud;
A third would cruise in a palace yacht like a red-
 necked prince of blood.
And so we dreamed and we vaunted, millionaires
 to a man,
Leaping to wealth in our visions long ere the
 trail began.

II.

We landed in wind-swept Skagway. We joined
 the weltering mass,
Clamoring over their outfits, waiting to climb
 the Pass.
We tightened our girths and our pack-straps; we
 linked on the Human Chain,
Struggling up to the summit, where every step
 was a pain.

Gone was the joy of our faces; grim and haggard
 and pale;
The heedless mirth of the shipboard was changed
 to the care of the trail.
We flung ourselves in the struggle, packing our
 grub in relays,
Step by step to the summit in the bale of the
 winter days.

Floundering deep in the sump-holes, stumbling out again;
Crying with cold and weakness, crazy with fear and pain.
Then from the depths of our travail, ere our spirits were broke,
Grim, tenacious and savage, the lust of the trail awoke.

"Klondike or bust!" rang the slogan; every man for his own.
Oh, how we flogged the horses, staggering skin and bone!
Oh, how we cursed their weakness, anguish they could not tell,
Breaking their hearts in our passion, lashing them on till they fell!

For grub meant gold to our thinking, and all that could walk must pack;
The sheep for the shambles stumbled, each with a load on its back;
And even the swine were burdened, and grunted and squealed and rolled,
And men went mad in the moment, huskily clamoring "Gold!"

Oh, we were brutes and devils, goaded by lust
 and fear!
Our eyes were strained to the Summit; the weaklings dropped to the rear,
Falling in heaps by the trail-side, heart-broken,
 limp and wan;
But the gaps closed up in an instant, and heedless the chain went on.

Never will I forget it, there on the mountain
 face,
Antlike, men with their burdens, clinging in icy
 space;
Dogged, determined and dauntless, cruel and
 callous and cold,
Cursing, blaspheming, reviling, and ever that
 battle-cry—" Gold!"

Thus toiled we, the army of fortune, in hunger
 and hope and despair,
Till glacier, mountain and forest vanished, and
 radiantly fair
There at our feet lay Lake Bennett, and down to
 its welcome we ran:
The trail of the land was over, the trail of the
 water began.

III.

We built our boats and we launched them. Never
    has been such a fleet;
A packing-case for a bottom, a mackinaw for a
    sheet.
Shapeless, grotesque, lopsided, flimsy, makeshift
    and crude,
Each man after his fashion builded as best he
    could.

Each man worked like a demon, as prow to rud-
    der we raced;
The winds of the Wild cried " Hurry," the voice
    of the waters, " Haste."
We hated those driving before us; we dreaded
    those pressing behind;
We cursed the slow current that bore us; we
    prayed to the God of the wind.

Spring! and the hillsides flourished, vivid in
    jeweled green;
Spring! and our hearts' blood nourished envy
    and hatred and spleen.
Little cared we for the Spring-birth; much cared
    we to get on—
Stake in the Great White Channel, stake ere the
    best be gone.

The greed of the gold possessed us; pity and
    love were forgot;
Covetous visions obsessed us; brother with
    brother fought.
Partner with partner wrangled, each one claim-
    ing his due;
Wrangled and halved their outfits, sawing their
    boats in two.

Thuswise we voyaged Lake Bennett, Tagish,
    then Windy Arm,
Sinister, savage and baleful, boding us hate and
    harm.
Many a scow was shattered, there on that iron
    shore;
Many a heart was broken, straining at sweep
    and oar.

We roused Lake Marsh with a chorus, we drifted
    many a mile;
There was the canyon before us—cave-like its
    dark defile;
The shores swept faster and faster; the river
    narrowed to wrath;
Waters that hissed disaster reared upright in our
    path.

Beneath us the green tumult churning, above us
  the cavernous gloom;
Around us, swift twisting and turning, the black,
  sullen walls of a tomb.
We spun like a chip in a mill-race; our hearts
  hammered under the test;
Then—oh, the relief on each chill face!—we
  soared into sunlight and rest.

Hand sought for hand on the instant. Cried we:
  "Our troubles are o'er."
Then, like a rumble of thunder, heard we a
  canorous roar.
Leaping and boiling and seething, saw we a
  cauldron afume;
There was the rage of the rapids, there was the
  menace of doom.

The river springs like a racer, sweeps through a
  gash in the rock;
Butts at the boulder-ribbed bottom, staggers and
  rears at the shock;
Leaps like a terrified monster, writhes in its fury
  and pain;
Then with the crash of a demon springs to the
  onset again.

Dared we that ravening terror; heard we its din
 in our ears;
Called on the God of our fathers, juggled forlorn with our fears;
Sank to our waists in its fury, tossed to the sky
 like a fleece;
Then, when our dread was the greatest, crashed
 into safety and peace.

But what of the others that followed, losing their
 boats by the score?
Well could we see them and hear them, strung
 down that desolate shore.
What of the poor souls that perished? Little of
 them shall be said—
On to the Golden Valley, pause not to bury the
 dead.

Then there were days of drifting, breezes soft as
 a sigh;
Night trailed her robe of jewels over the floor of
 the sky.
The moonlit stream was a python, silver, sinuous,
 vast,
That writhed on a shroud of velvet—well, it was
 done at last.

There were the tents of Dawson, there the scar
 of the slide;
Swiftly we poled o'er the shallows, swiftly leapt
 o'er the side.
Fires fringed the mouth of Bonanza; sunset
 gilded the dome;
The test of the trail was over—thank God, thank
 God, we were Home!

Clancy of the Mounted Police

In the little Crimson Manual it's written plain
 and clear
That who would wear the scarlet coat shall say
 good-bye to fear;
Shall be a guardian of the right, a sleuth-hound
 of the trail—
In the little Crimson Manual there's no such
 word as " fail "—
Shall follow on though heavens fall, or hell's
 top-turrets freeze,
Half round the world, if need there be, on bleed-
 ing hands and knees.
It's duty, duty, first and last, the Crimson
 Manual saith;
The Scarlet Rider makes reply: " It's duty—to
 the death."
And so they sweep the solitudes, free men from
 all the earth;

And so they sentinel the woods, the wilds that
 know their worth;
And so they scour the startled plains and mock
 at hurt and pain,
And read their Crimson Manual, and find their
 duty plain.
Knights of the lists of unrenown, born of the
 frontier's need,
Disdainful of the spoken word, exultant in the
 deed;
Unconscious heroes of the waste, proud players
 of the game;
Props of the power behind the Throne, upholders
 of the name:
For thus the Great White Chief hath said, "In
 all my lands be peace,"
And to maintain his word he gave his West the
 Scarlet Police.

Livid-lipped was the valley, still as the grave of
 God;
 Misty shadows of mountain thinned into mists
  of cloud;
Corpselike and stark was the land, with a quiet
 that crushed and awed,
 And the stars of the weird Sub-arctic glim-
  mered over its shroud.

Deep in the trench of the valley two men stationed the Post,
  Seymour and Clancy the reckless, fresh from the long patrol;
Seymour, the sergeant, and Clancy, Clancy who made his boast
  He could cinch like a broncho the Northland, and cling to the prongs of the Pole.

Two lone men on detachment, standing for law on the trail;
  Undismayed in the vastness, wise with the wisdom of old—
Out of the night hailed a half-breed, telling a pitiful tale,
  "White man starving and crazy on the banks of the Nordenscold."

Up sprang the red-haired Clancy, lean and eager of eye;
  Loaded the long toboggan, strapped each dog at its post;
Whirled his lash at the leader; then, with a whoop and a cry,
  Into the Great White Silence faded away like a ghost.

The clouds were a misty shadow, the hills were
    a shadowy mist;
  Sunless, voiceless and pulseless, the day was a
      dream of woe
Through the ice-rifts the river smoked and
    bubbled and hissed;
  Behind was a trail fresh broken, in front the
      untrodden snow.

Ahead of the dogs ploughed Clancy, haloed by
    steaming breath;
  Through peril of open water, through ache of
      insensate cold;
Up rivers wantonly winding in a land affianced
    to death,
  Till he came to a cowering cabin on the banks
      of the Nordenscold.

Then Clancy loosed his revolver, and he strode
    through the open door;
  And there was the man he sought for, crouch-
      ing beside the fire;
The hair of his beard was singeing, the frost on
    his back was hoar,
  And ever he crooned and chanted as if he never
      would tire:

"I panned and I panned in the shiny sand, and
    I sniped on the river bar;
But I know, I know, that it's down below that
    the golden treasures are;
So I'll wait and wait till the floods abate, and I'll
    sink a shaft once more,
And I'd like to bet that I'll go home yet with a
    brass band playing on before."

He was nigh as thin as a sliver, and he whined
    like a moose-hide cur;
  So Clancy clothed him and nursed him as a
      mother nurses a child;
Lifted him on the toboggan, wrapped him in
    robes of fur,
  Then with the dogs sore straining, started to
      face the Wild.

Said the Wild: "I will crush this Clancy, so
    fearless and insolent;
  For him will I loose my fury, and blind and
      buffet and beat;
Pile up my snows to stay him; then when his
    strength is spent,
  Leap on him from my ambush and crush him
      under my feet.

"Him will I ring with my silence, compass him
   with my cold;
  Closer and closer clutch him unto mine icy
   breast;
Buffet him with my blizzards, deep in my snow
   enfold,
  Claiming his life as my tribute, giving my
   wolves the rest."

Clancy crawled through the vastness; o'er him
   the hate of the Wild;
  Full on his face fell the blizzard; cheering his
   huskies he ran;
Fighting, fierce-hearted and tireless, snows that
   drifted and piled,
  With ever and ever behind him singing the
   crazy man:

*" Sing hey, sing ho, for the ice and snow,
  And a heart that's ever merry;
Let us trim and square with a lover's care
  (For why should a man be sorry?)
A grave deep, deep, with the moon a-peep.
  A grave in the frozen mould.
Sing hey, sing ho, for the winds that blow,
And a grave deep down in the ice and snow,
  A grave in the land of gold."*

Day after day of darkness, the whirl of the seeth-
    ing snows;
  Day after day of blindness, the swoop of the
    stinging blast;
On through a blur of fury, the swing of stagger-
    ing blows;
  On through a world of turmoil, empty, inane
    and vast.

Night with its writhing storm-whirl, night des-
    pairingly black;
  Night with its hours of terror, numb and end-
    lessly long;
Night with its weary waiting, fighting the
    shadows back,
  And ever the crouching madman singing his
    crazy song.

Cold with its creeping terror, cold with its sud-
    den clinch;
  Cold so utter you wonder if 'twill ever again
    be warm;
Clancy grinned as he shuddered, "Surely it
    isn't a cinch
  Being wet-nurse to a looney in the teeth of an
    Arctic storm."

The blizzard passed and the dawn broke, knife-
    edged and crystal-clear;
  The sky was a blue-domed iceberg, sunshine
    outlawed away;
Ever by snowslide and ice-rip haunted and
    hovered the Fear;
  Ever the Wild malignant poised and panted
    to slay.

The lead-dog freezes in harness—cut him out of
    the team!
  The lung of the wheel-dog's bleeding—shoot
    him and let him lie;
On and on with the others—lash them until they
    scream;
  "Pull for your lives, you devils! On! To
    halt is to die."

There in the frozen vastness Clancy fought with
    his foes;
  The ache of the stiffened fingers, the cut of the
    snowshoe thong;
Cheeks black-raw through the hood-flap, eyes
    that tingled and closed;
  And ever to urge and cheer him quavered the
    madman's song.

Colder it grew and colder, till the last heat left
   the earth,
 And there in the great stark stillness the bale
    fires glinted and gleamed,
And the Wild all around exulted and shook with
   a devilish mirth,
 And life was far and forgotten, the ghost of a
    joy once dreamed.

Death! And one who defied it, a man of the
   Mounted Police;
 Fought it there to a standstill long after hope
    was gone;
Grinned through his bitter anguish, fought without let or cease,
 Suffering, straining, striving, stumbling,
    struggling on.

Till the dogs lay down in their traces, and rose
   and staggered and fell;
 Till the eyes of him dimmed with shadows, and
    the trail was so hard to see;
Till the Wild howled out triumphant, and the
   world was a frozen hell—
 Then said Constable Clancy: "I guess that
    it's up to me."

Far down the trail they saw him, and his hands
    they were blanched like bone;
  His face was a blackened horror, from his eye-
    lids the salt rheum ran;
His feet he was lifting strangely, as if they were
    made of stone,
  But safe in his arms, and sleeping, he carried
    the crazy man.

So Clancy got into Barracks, and the boys made
    rather a scene;
  And the O. C. called him a hero, and was nice
    as a man could be;
But Clancy gazed down his trousers at the place
    where his toes had been,
  And then he howled like a husky, and sang in
    a shaky key:

*" When I go back to the old love that's true to the
    finger-tips,*
*I'll say: ' Here's bushels of gold, love,' and I'll
    kiss my girl on the lips;*
*' It's yours to have and to hold, love.' It's the
    proud, proud boy I will be,*
*When I go back to the old love that's waited so
    long for me."*

Lost

"BLACK *is the sky, but the land is white—*
  (*O, the wind, the snow and the storm*).
Father, where is our boy to-night?
  Pray to God he is safe and warm."

"*Mother, mother, why should you fear?*
  Safe is he, and the Arctic moon
Over his cabin shines so clear—
  Rest and sleep, 'twill be morning soon."

"It's getting dark awful sudden. Say, this is
     mighty queer!
  Where in the world have I got to? It's still
     and black as a tomb.
I reckoned the camp was yonder, I figured the
     trail was here—
  Nothing! just draw and valley packed with
     quiet and gloom;
Snow that comes down like feathers, thick and
     gobby and grey;

Lost

Night that looks spiteful ugly—seems that I've
    lost my way.

"The cold's got an edge like a jack-knife—it
    must be forty below;
  Leastways that's what it seems like—it cuts so
    fierce to the bone.
The wind's getting real ferocious; it's heaving
    and whirling the snow;
  It swings with a howl of fury, it dies away to
    a moan;
Its arms sweep around like a banshee's, swift
    and icily white,
And buffet and blind and beat me. Lord! It's a
    hell of a night!

"I'm all tangled up in a blizzard. There's
    only one thing to do—
  Keep on moving and moving; it's death, it's
    death if I rest.
Oh, God! if I see the morning, if only I struggle
    through,
  I'll say the prayers I've forgotten since I lay
    on my mother's breast.
I seem going round in a circle; maybe the camp
    is near,
  Say! Did somebody holler? Was it a light
    I saw?

Or was it only a notion? I'll shout, and maybe
    they'll hear—
  No! the wind only drowns me—shout till my
    throat is raw.

" The boys are all round the camp-fire wondering
    when I'll be back.
  They'll soon be starting to seek me, they'll
    scarcely wait for the light.
What will they find, I wonder, when they come
    to the end of my track—
  A hand stuck out of a snowdrift, frozen and
    stiff and white?
That's what they'll strike, I reckon; that's how
    they'll find their pard,
  A pie-faced corpse in a snowbank—curse you,
    don't be a fool!
Play the game to the finish; bet on your very
    last card;
  Nerve yourself for the struggle. Oh, you
    coward, keep cool!

" I'm going to lick this blizzard; I'm going to
    live the night.
  It can't down me with its bluster—I'm not the
    kind to be beat.

On hands and knees will I buck it; with every
    breath will I fight;
  It's life, it's life that I fight for—never it
    seemed so sweet.
I know that my face is frozen; my hands are
    numblike and dead;
  But oh, my feet keep a-moving, heavy and hard
    and slow;
They're trying to kill me, kill me, the night that's
    black overhead,
  The wind that cuts like a razor, the whipcord
    lash of the snow.
Keep a-moving, a-moving; don't, don't stumble,
    you fool!
  Curse this snow that's a-piling a-purpose to
    block my way.
It's heavy as gold in the rocker, it's white and
    fleecy as wool;
  It's soft as a bed of feathers, it's warm as a
    stack of hay.
Curse on my feet that slip so, my poor, tired,
    stumbling feet;
  I guess they're a job for the surgeon, they feel
    so queerlike to lift.
I'll rest them just for a moment—oh, but to rest
    is sweet;
  The awful wind cannot get me, deep, deep
    down in the drift."

Lost

" Father, a bitter cry I heard,
  Out of the night so dark and wild.
Why is my heart so strangely stirred?
  'Twas like the voice of our erring child."

" Mother, mother, you only heard
  A waterfowl in the locked lagoon;
Out of the night a wounded bird—
  Rest and sleep, 'twill be morning soon."

" Who is it talks of sleeping? I'll swear that somebody shook
  Me hard by the arm for a moment, but how on earth could it be?
See how my feet are moving—awfully funny they look—
  Moving as if they belonged to a someone that wasn't me.
The wind down the night's long alley bowls me down like a pin;
  I stagger and fall and stagger, crawl arm-deep in the snow.
Beaten back to my corner, how can I hope to win?
  And there is the blizzard waiting to give me the knockout blow.

"Oh, I'm so warm and sleepy; no more hunger and pain.
  Just to rest for a moment; was ever rest such a joy?
Ha, what was that? I'll swear it! Somebody shook me again;
  Somebody seemed to whisper: "Fight to the last, my boy."
Fight! that's right, I must struggle. I know that to rest means death.
  Death! but then what does death mean?—ease from a world of strife.
Life has been none too pleasant; yet with my failing breath
  Still and still must I struggle, fight for the gift of life.

* * * * * * *

Seems that I must be dreaming; here is the old home trail;
  Yonder a light is gleaming; oh, I know it so well!
The air is scented with clover; the cattle wait by the rail;
  Father is through with the milking; there goes the supper bell.

* * * * * * *

Mother, your boy is crying, out in the night and
    cold;
  Let me in and forgive me, I'll never be bad
    any more;
I'm oh, so sick and so sorry; please, dear mother,
    don't scold—
  It's just your boy, and he wants you . . . .
    Mother, open the door. . . ."

   *   *   *   *   *   *   *

" Father, father, I saw a face
  Pressed just now to the window-pane!
Oh, it gazed for a moment's space,
  Wild and wan, and was gone again."

" Mother, mother, you saw the snow
  Drifted down from the maple tree.
(Oh, the wind that is sobbing so—
  Weary and worn and old are we)—
Only the snow and a wounded loon—
Rest and sleep, 'twill be morning soon."

L'Envoi

We talked of yesteryears, of trails and treasure,
    Of men who played the game and lost or won;
Of mad stampedes, of toil beyond all measure,
    Of campfire comfort when the day was done.
We talked of sullen nights by moon-dogs haunted,
    Of bird and beast and tree, of rod and gun;
Of boat and tent, of hunting trip enchanted
    Beneath the wonder of the midnight sun;
Of bloody-footed dogs that gnawed the traces,
    Of prisoned seas, wind-lashed and winter-locked:
The ice-grey dawn was pale upon our faces,
    Yet still we filled the cup and still we talked.

The city street was dimmed. We saw the glitter
    Of moon-picked brilliants on the virgin snow,
And down the drifted canyon heard the bitter
    Relentless slogan of the winds of woe.

L'Envoi

The city was forgot, and parka-skirted
  We trod that leagueless land that once we knew;
We saw stream past down valleys glacier-girted
  The wolf-worn legions of the caribou.
We smoked our pipes, o'er scenes of triumph dwelling;
  Of deeds of daring, dire defeats we talked;
And other tales that lost not in the telling,
  Ere to our beds uncertainly we walked.

And so, dear friends, in gentler valleys roaming,
  Perhaps, when on my printed page you look,
Your fancies by the firelight may go homing
  To that lone land that haply you forsook.
And if, perchance, you hear the silence calling,
  The frozen music of star-yearning heights,
Or, dreaming, see the seines of silver trawling
  Across the sky's abyss on vasty nights,
You may recall that sweep of savage splendor,
  That land that measures each man at his worth,
And feel in memory, half fierce, half tender,
  The brotherhood of men that know the North.

CPSIA information can be obtained
at www.ICGtesting.com
Printed in the USA
LVHW061056290821
696378LV00002B/61